World History Map Workbook
Second Edition

Geographical and Critical Thinking Exercises

Volume 1 – to 1600

Glee E. Wilson
Kent State University

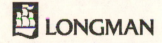 **LONGMAN**

An Imprint of Addison Wesley Longman, Inc.

New York • Reading, Massachusetts • Menlo Park, California • Harlow, England
Don Mills, Ontario • Sydney • Mexico City • Madrid • Amsterdam

World History Map Workbook, *second edition,* **Volume 1 – to 1600**

Copyright © 2000 by Addison Wesley Longman, Inc.

Please visit our website at http://www.awlonline.com

ISBN: 0-321-06632-4

345678910 – VG- 03 02

CONTENTS

Introduction   v

I   An Introduction to the Elements of the Earth   1
II   Early Humans in Sub-Saharan Africa   8
III   The Beginnings of Civilization in the Ancient Near East:
           City-States and International Empires   12
IV   Early Civilization in Ancient Egypt   14
V   Israel, Judah, the Ancient Hebrews, and Their Neighbors   21
VI   The Age of Empires: Babylonia, Assyria, Persia   25
VII   Early Civilization in India   29
VIII   Early China   33
IX   Early Civilization in Middle and South America   37
X   The Early Aegean   41
XI   Ancient Greece   45
XII   Alexander the Great and the Hellenistic Age   49
XIII   China's Struggle for Cultural and Political Unity, 400 B.C.–A.D. 400   55
XIV   India, CA. 700–200 B.C.: Kingdoms and Empire   59
XV   Rome, Italy and Empire   63
XVI   Rome, Byzantium and the Barbarians   67
XVII   Arab Expansion and the Islamic World, A.D. 570–800   71
XVIII   Islam and Africa: East and West, A.D. 1000–1500   77
XIX   T'ang China: Unity and Expansion, A.D. 618–907   83
XX   Political Regionalism and Cultural Unity in the
           Gupta-Harsha Eras, A.D. 400–650   87
XXI   Southeast Asia, Japan and Korea   93
XXII   The Carolingian Empire   99
XXIII   New Formations in Europe: Saxons, Slavs, Magyars,
           Vikings, and Saracens   105
XXIV   The Early Middle Ages: Emperors,
           Kings and Crusaders, A.D. 1000–1300   111
XXV   The High Middle Ages: Kingdoms and Empires, 1200–1500   117
XXVI   Sung (Song) China, The Mongols, Ming China, and Imperial Japan   123
XXVII   Renaissance Italy: 1400–1600   129
XXVIII   Discovery and Exploration I: Africa   133
XXIX   Discovery and Exploration II: "The New World"   139
XXX   The Islamic World: The Ottoman Empire   145
XXXI   The World of Islam: Iran, India, and North Africa   151
XXXII   The World of Islam: India and Southeast Asia   157
XXXIII   Europe, CA. 1600   163

INTRODUCTION

On July 20, 1969, the American astronaut Neil Armstrong set foot on the moon. A prominent broadcast journalist commented on the occasion that this was indeed a momentous achievement. He went on to say that the lunar landing was even more significant than Columbus's discoveries in the Americas. The television anchorman, in his justifiable excitement and enthusiasm over a significant technical accomplishment, may have overlooked a number of important points.

The astronauts knew where they were going and how to return. They knew the exact distances they would travel on their trip. They knew how to achieve their objectives and they succeeded in heroic fashion. What is more, they knew for the most part what they would find upon arrival. They found no "man in the moon," and no little green men greeted their landing craft. And, of course, they were not at all surprised to find that the moon was not made of green cheese.

Perhaps the real significance of the moon landing was that we beat the Russians to it. Political motives were at the base of this great scientific, technical, and national achievement.

The earthbound Genoese Christopher Columbus, on the other hand, was looking for an alternative route to the East Indies. Instead, he came upon a group of islands in the Caribbean Sea which would be called the West Indies. Columbus was correct in his assumption that, given the Earth was a globe, one could discover the routes to the riches of the East by sailing west from Europe.

Political, national and economic motives were at work here, too. Ferdinand and Isabella of Spain supported Columbus after he had been turned down by John II of Portugal. The Spanish monarchs faced the possibilities of losing the race to the East after the Portuguese took another route south around Africa and then east across the Indian Ocean. Columbus was correct, in general, but his calculations with respect to the time and distances involved were off. But the major significance of his voyages and those that followed lay in the discovery and exploration of lands, peoples, and cultures of which the Europeans were completely ignorant. Ironically, Columbus persisted until his death in the belief that he had reached the East.

In any case, it was only a short time until the true dimensions of the European voyages would unfold. The continents, the islands, the bodies of water, and the varieties of indigenous peoples and cultures came as a complete shock to those who were expecting to come upon India and China. Neither history, tradition, nor their science prepared them for what they found. Their history, geography, and theology now required reevaluation. Just as the recent advances in astronomy and the understanding of the mechanics of our solar system challenged the Ptolemaic and Biblical authorities, the fifteenth and sixteenth century voyages of exploration and discovery called for a profound reassessment of the Judeo-Christian Eurocentric views on human creation and human history.

What started out, in part, as a reaction to the Ottoman Turkish Empire's disruption of traditional trade routes would have tremendous significance for Europe and the world at large. The impact on the "discovered" lands and peoples is a major part of the equation, of course. In the fifteenth century, Europe, the Americas, Africa, and Asia were caught up in a process of transformation that continues to this day.

The repercussions over the past five centuries, and especially the relatively recent developments in the post-colonial world, dominate contemporary political and economic issues. The most basic checklist of key countries and regions must include China, India, Africa, Indonesia, Southeast Asia, etc. In the Americas, Quebec, the Panama Canal, Cuba, Nicaragua, and Mexico come to mind immediately when topics of cultural identity, economic opportunity, political boundaries, and international affairs are raised. The recent five hundredth anniversary of Columbus's voyages in 1492 provoked a variety of issues such as race, slavery, genocide, and cultural imperialism.

The events connected with the Spanish, Portuguese, Dutch, English and French activities outside Europe illustrate in a dramatic way the connection of history and geography, requiring evaluation and analysis based on knowledge. The important element is the human context . . . the human perspective and its significance in human history.

The causes, consequences and historical significance of the eleventh century Viking encounters in the New World and the undeniably impressive early fifteenth century Chinese voyages of Cheng Ho, require evaluation. These voyages amounted to little in the long run. The Viking adventures in the Western Hemisphere might have been largely accidental. The Chinese motivations are well-documented and their reaction to contacts in Africa and India were typically conservative and chauvinistic.

In contrast, the Portuguese interest in Africa was soon heightened by the prospect of slaves and gold and enhanced by posts at the Cape of Good Hope as stepping-stones to the East. The Spanish route to the West turned up unimagined surprises in the form of two unknown continents, a vast number of islands, and the huge Pacific Ocean. The bonus of millions of new subjects to be utilized as labor and won over to Christianity added to the windfall for the Crown and Church.

Today, Africa is home to fifty-two countries, North and Central America to twenty-three, and South America to thirteen. And it is a rare one that is not inextricably bound up in the greater political and economic global scheme of things.

The recent spectacular achievements of the space age such as the lunar landing, scientific experiments conducted in the space shuttle missions, and satellite-based deep space explorations have not altered the reality that human beings are earthbound. New satellite-based techniques have resulted in the extremely complete and accurate mapping of the Earth's surface. The Earth remains, for the present at least, the focus or base of virtually all human history. The space race between the USA and the USSR, so important in the post–World War II years, seems now to have given way to potentially productive cooperative endeavors. The motivations were and remain human- and Earth-centered. Intellectual curiosity, political and economic competition, intelligence-gathering and construction of missile launch platforms continue to be motivated from and focused on our Earth.

Any understanding of past, present, or future human activity requires a basic knowledge of the main geographical features of our planet. Human history takes place within a chronological dimension in the context of the earthly spatial dimension. Geography is the discipline that focuses on place or location in the physical dimension. There always has been a close, but not necessarily deterministic relationship between human activity and the physical elements of the Earth. The human struggle for survival, the history of civilization, and the physical world are closely interrelated.

USE OF THE WORKBOOK

The exercises in this workbook are designed to assist in the understanding of the relationships between human activity and the physical and topographic features of the Earth. This workbook is aimed at a critical and analytical approach to the key eras, places, and regions in the human experience. There is no presumption of advanced knowledge of geography or cartographic skills.

The workbook does, however, stress elements other than the simple copy-book transfer of place names from one map to an outline format. The assignments take the student through the process of reading maps, making maps, and interpreting maps which correlate with various phases in the development of civilization.

The assignments require the student to locate, identify, label, and interpret physical and man-made features in conjunction with a thoughtful reading of a survey text. The introductory statement for each exercise summarizes major themes. Among other things, it will be important to take note of the land masses, bodies of water, river systems, and other topographic features such as mountain chains, deserts, and general vegetation patterns.

General observations on climate, weather, rainfall patterns and their impact on human history can be extrapolated as the exercises proceed. The location, control, exploration, and distribution of such natural resources as minerals, timber, oil, gas, game, and fish, are additional themes that naturally come to mind as appropriate for consideration in many of the exercises.

ORGANIZATION OF EXERCISES

The exercises are made up of three parts. Part I calls for the location of major bodies of water (oceans, seas, lakes, river systems), mountain chains, historical and political boundaries, as well as cities. Part II of the exercise is designed to result in an awareness of the relationships of various geographical and man-made features to political, cultural, and economic factors. Part III of the exercise has the object of correlating features from the map to the narrative of the text. This three-step process involves the student in a critical and analytical process that combines and refines several skills.

RECOMMENDATIONS

Successful completion of these exercises requires the use of some basic cartographic techniques. In order to read and make a map, one should note and use the scale (inches to miles), the parallels of latitude measured 0°-90° north and south of the Equator, and meridians of longitude, measured 0°-180° east and west of the Greenwich Prime Meridian. Please bear in mind that distortions in size, proportions, and perspective occur when the shapes on a globe are transferred to the flat surface of a map. **IN THE INTEREST OF CLARITY AND ACCURACY, IT MAY BE USEFUL TO MAKE AN ENLARGED DUPLICATE FOR A WORK COPY AS WELL AS A FINAL COPY. ALSO, YOU MAY WANT TO MAKE ADDITIONAL COPIES OF THE OUTLINE MAP AND USE A SEPARATE ONE FOR THE LOCATION OF CITIES, BOUNDARIES, RIVERS, OR OTHER ITEMS CALLED FOR IN THE ASSIGNMENT.** Proper completion of the exercises requires a good-quality, hard lead pencil, a set of color pencils, a ruler, and an inexpensive compass.

ACKNOWLEDGMENTS

Among the works consulted, the following have been particularly useful: G. Barraclough, *The Times Atlas of World History* (London, 1991); H. Kinder and W. Hilgermann, *The Penguin Atlas of World History* (London, 1978); P. Vidal-Naquet, *The Harper Atlas of World History* (New York, 1987); C. Scarre, *Past Worlds: The Times Atlas of Archaeology* (Maplewood, N.J., 1988); M. Wise and G. Motta, *The Great Geographical Atlas* (New York, 1991); M. S. Hoffman, *The World Almanac and Book of Facts* (New York, 1993); G. J. Demko, *Why in the World: Adventures in Geography* (New York, 1992); P.R. Magocsi, *Historical Atlas of East Central Europe* (Seattle, 1993); J. Keegan, *The Times Atlas of the Second World War* (London, 1989); and the *Hammond Universal World Atlas* (Maplewood, New Jersey, 1993).

I. AN INTRODUCTION TO THE ELEMENTS OF THE EARTH

Geography is one of the most important sister disciplines of history. The study, interpretation, and analysis of human activity in time and space are closely interwoven. The physical disposition of land masses, bodies of water, and topographical features of the Earth have had an impact directly and indirectly on human achievement since our earliest ancestors appeared on the planet. A balanced view of the long span of mankind's development requires a basic knowledge of the physical components of the Earth. In our "global era" the spatial perspective is even more important as we are confronted with continuing traditional political and economic issues in the competition for territory and resources.

The contemporary problems of nuclear and other toxic pollutants in the atmosphere, soil, and water supply have resulted in a worldwide crisis. Waste disposal and the depletion of such natural resources as fresh water, productive soil, rain forests, and fuel supplies threaten civilization, and the planet itself.

Recalling certain basic features and their interrelationships is helpful as we examine the human realm and its relationship to the physical or topographic realm. An introductory exercise will promote an understanding of basic components and the dynamic nature of the planet. It is useful to recall, for instance, that the seven continents, the mountain chains, deserts, forests, oceans, seas, and lakes that appear neatly placed on a simplified flat map or globe are the result of hundreds of millions of years of development. The Earth, one of seven planets in our solar system, is about 4.5 billion years old.

The continents, which make up only about thirty percent of the Earth's surface are moving apart about three-quarters of an inch a year. This movement, referred to as continental drift, began somewhere around 225 million years ago. In about fifty million years substantial parts of East Africa and the west coast of North America will separate from their continents as a result of this process. At that time, the Mediterranean Sea will disappear, the Atlantic Ocean will be larger and the Pacific smaller.

In the shorter term, the relatively recent glacial era, and still more recent catastrophic flooding, droughts, volcanic eruptions, and earthquakes have had their effects on the Earth and its flora and fauna. And, it is necessary to recall such man-made abuses as the Exxon Valdez oil spill, the Chernobyl nuclear disaster, and the threat of global warming (or cooling).

Consider, as well, that over thirty percent of the land surface is covered by desert, not including the substantial cold-desert area of the polar and sub-polar regions. And slightly over ten percent of the remaining land mass is covered by glaciers. Finally, of course, about seventy percent of the Earth's surface is covered by water. The sub-surface regions of the Earth's oceans remain largely unexplored. Today, they are man's last frontier on Earth. The tremendous potential of underseas mineral and nutritional resources is now on the agenda for human development. Any systematic approach to the history of civilization calls for a global, historical, chronological, and geographical perspective.

EXERCISE 1
AN INTRODUCTION TO THE ELEMENTS OF THE EARTH

I.   MAKING THE MAP (Two Maps)

1.   Locate and label North America, Central America, South America.
2.   Locate and label Antarctica and Australia.
3.   Locate and label Asia, Africa, Europe.
4.   Locate and label the Atlantic Ocean, the Indian Ocean, the Pacific Ocean, the Mediterranean Sea, the Black Sea, the Caspian Sea.
5.   Locate and label the Red Sea, the Bering Sea, the North Sea, the Baltic Sea, the China Sea, the Arabian Sea, the Persian Gulf, the Gulf of Mexico.
6.   Locate and label the English Channel, The Strait of Gibraltar, the Suez Canal, the Panama Canal.
7.   Locate and label the Rocky Mountains, the Andes Mountains, the Alps Mountains, the Himalaya Mountains, the Ural Mountains.
8.   Locate and label the Equator, the Tropic of Capricorn, the Tropic of Cancer.

II.   READING THE MAP

1.   The Nile River is located in what continent?
2.   What is the major river system in Brazil?
3.   What is the longest river system in the United States?
4.   Name two major rivers that empty into the Black Sea.
5.   The Tigris and Euphrates rivers are located in _____ and empty into the _____ Gulf.
6.   Two major rivers in the Indian subcontinent are the _____ on the west and the _____ in the east.
7.   The two major river systems in China are the _____ and the _____. Both flow to the _____.
8.   The Rhine and the Danube rivers located on the continent of _____ flow generally to the _____ and _____ respectively.

III.   UNDERSTANDING THE MAP

1.   Name the two largest nations in the North America today.
2.   Name the large series of islands located off the northeast coast of China.
3.   What complex of islands is located off the west coast of Europe?
4.   Name the five largest islands in the Mediterranean Sea.
5.   Name the three largest islands due south off the coast of Florida.
6.   What are the two largest continents on the Earth?
7.   What bodies of water are connected by the Panama Canal?

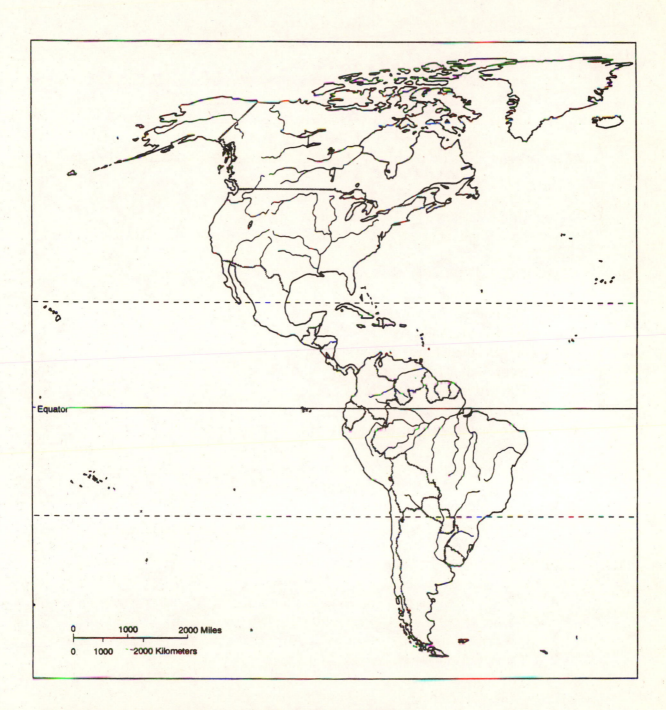

Equator

| 0 | 1000 | 2000 Miles |
| 0 | 1000 | 2000 Kilometers |

Exercise 1: An Introduction to the Elements of the Earth

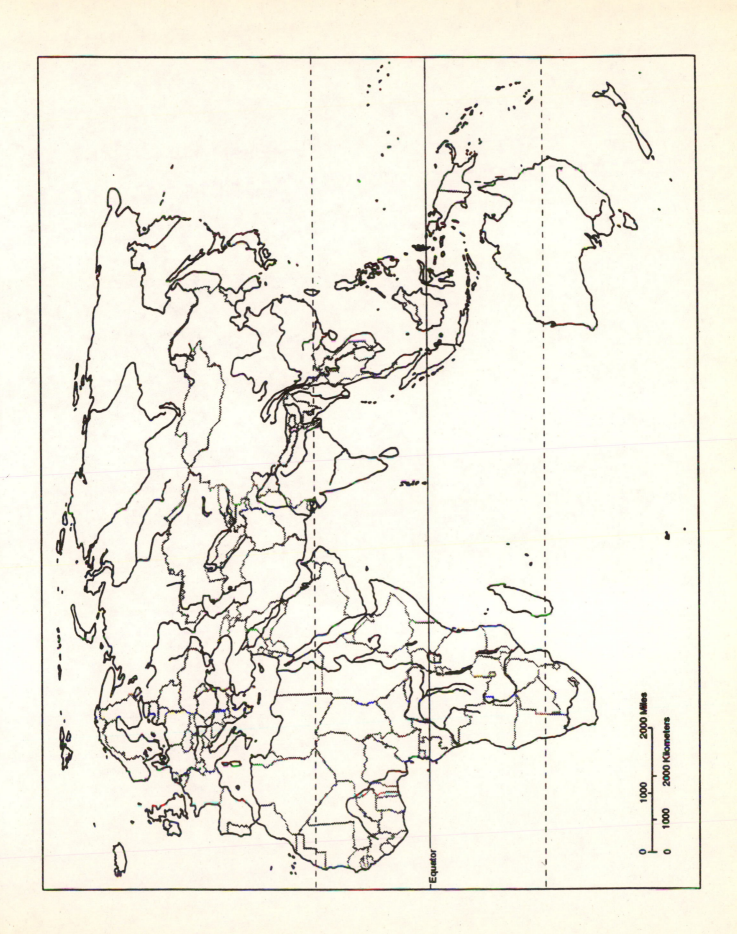

Equator

2000 Miles

1000

0

2000 Kilometers

1000

1000

0

II. EARLY HUMANS IN SUB-SAHARAN AFRICA

Africa is the world's second largest continent after Asia. Overall it comprises twenty percent of the Earth's surface. It is estimated that its population will exceed one and a half billion (equal to that of North and South America and Europe combined) by 2025. It is bounded on the north by the Mediterranean Sea, on the east by the Indian Ocean and the Red Sea, and by the Atlantic to the west. At its extremities, it measures about 5,000 miles from Tunis to Cape Town north to south. From east to west, the direct overland distance from Cape Guardafir on the Somali Peninsula to Cape Verde is even greater at approximately 5,500 miles. This vast continent is connected to Asia in northeast Egypt at the Sinai Peninsula. Africa is bisected by the Equator and extends well beyond the Tropic of Cancer to the north and the Tropic of Capricorn to the south.

There are five distinct climate zones which encompass the extremes of high mountains, deserts, swamps, and dense tropical rain forests as well as savannahs and the fertile and temperate lowlands. Its geography, topography, and geologic history are as rich and varied as its abundant flora, fauna, and natural resources. The Nile is only one of five major river systems and there are at least as many large deserts.

Among the various mountain chains, the highest peak of Kilimanjaro exceeds 19,000 feet, surpassed in the United States only by Mount McKinley. Active volcanoes are quite common in Central and West African ranges. The Great Rift System of East Central Africa is geologically active and complex, having been formed by volcanic uplift and faulting. African rivers, with the exception of the Nile, are not conducive to travel, commerce, or communication.

The deserts (the Sahara alone makes up about one-third of Africa's land area), swamps, and rain forests further inhibit trade and migration and encourage isolation of various regions and cultures. The irregular rainfall patterns, which swing from years of drought to long periods of intense rainfall, have a devastating effect on agriculture through soil depletion and erosion. Another ever-present negative factor in African development has been the decimating impact of insect pests and parasitic and tropical diseases on man, agriculture, and domestic animals.

It is in what is now called the Rift Valley that the earliest remains of *hominids* have been found. Several millions of years ago, in what is now Ethiopia, Kenya, and Tanzania, early man's ancestors originated. Cereal production and animal husbandry developed in various regions of Africa as humans moved from hunting and gathering economies. Agricultural practices may have originated very early in Nubia or Egypt. The coast of North Africa, Ethiopia, the Sudan, and the western area of the Upper Niger are regions where the record of such development is clear. The encroaching desert and the search for better soil and water supplies resulted in long periods of migration for such groups as the Bantu until their settlement in sub-Saharan Africa. In East Africa, Kush and Ethiopia followed Egypt as important kingdoms.

EXERCISE 2
EARLY HUMANS IN SUB-SAHARAN AFRICA

I. MAKING THE MAP

1. Locate and label the Atlantic Ocean, the Indian Ocean, the Red Sea, the Mediterranean Sea, the Gulf of Aden, the Gulf of Guinea.
2. Locate and label the Sahara Desert, the Kalahari Desert, the Namibian Desert.
3. Locate and label the Atlas Mountains, the Rift Valley, the Ethiopian Highlands, Olduvai Gorge.
4. Locate and label the Nile River, the Congo River, the Niger River, the Benue River, the Senegal River, the Zambezi River, the Orange River, the Vaal River.
5. Locate and label Lake Chad, Lake Malawi, Lake Victoria, Lake Tanganyika.
6. Draw the line of the Equator on the map.

II. READING THE MAP

1. The area of the Sahara Desert is approximately _____ square miles.
2. The Congo River empties into what body of water? _____
3. The Nile River flows from _____ to _____ and empties into the _____ Sea.
4. The two major desert areas in the south of Africa are the _____ and the _____.
5. The Benue River flows into the _____ River and eventually into the Gulf of _____.

III. UNDERSTANDING THE MAP

1. Where was the original Bantu homeland located?
2. What was the cause of the major climate change that affected Africa about ten thousand years ago and what impact did it have in the Saharan/Sudanic regions?
3. In general, what are the climatic and ecological conditions of Equatorial Africa?
4. Approximately how much of Africa can be described as tropical rain forest and where is it concentrated?

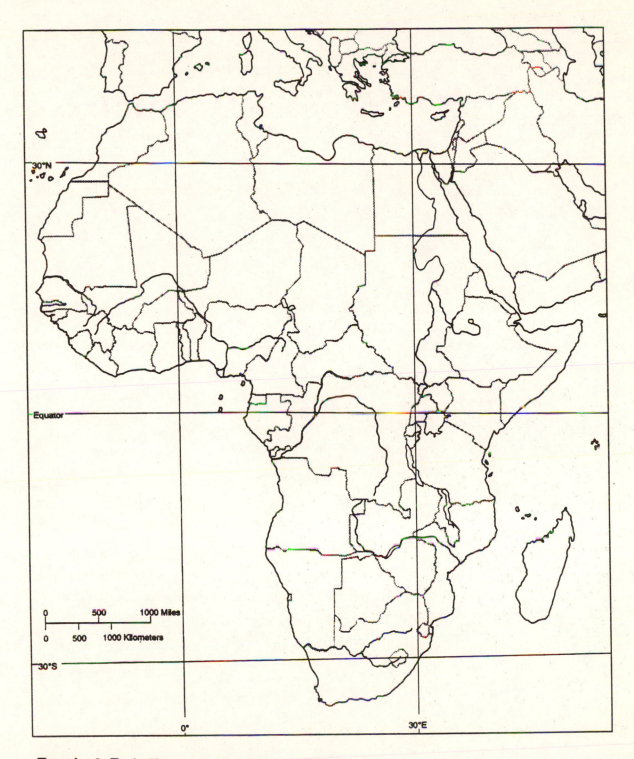

Exercise 2: Early Humans in Sub-Saharan Africa

III. THE BEGINNINGS OF CIVILIZATION IN THE ANCIENT NEAR EAST: CITY-STATES AND INTERNATIONAL EMPIRES

In the region traditionally referred to as the Near East or Western Asia, protoneolithic technologies resulted in the development of a variety of agricultural patterns. In rain-fed areas and eventually in the alluvial plains of large river systems, potential for urban and territorial states was established. As early as the ninth millennium from Syria and Palestine in the west to the foothills of the Zagros Mountains in the east, communities broadened their opportunities as they supplemented hunting and gathering and nomadic patterns with the harvesting of wild grains and eventually moved to true agriculture. In the hostile Syrian Desert at Jericho, the Konya plain north of the Taurus Mountains at Catal Hüyük in central Anatolia, and in the upper Tigris and Euphrates River valleys, human ingenuity and generations of experience brought together the essential ingredients of the beginnings of civilization. The lessons learned in northern and central Mesopotamia (Iraq) at Halaf and Ubaid, for instance, proved revolutionary when applied in the region to the south which came to be Sumer. The revolutionary developments occured as early as the fourth millennium B.C.

The Tigris flows southeast for over one thousand miles before it joins the Euphrates to its west, eventually emptying into the Persian Gulf. The Euphrates begins far to the north, beyond Lake Van and swings to the west in its 1600 mile journey southward.

The urban civilization that began in Sumer depended on advanced agriculture, complex irrigation systems, and wide-ranging foreign trade. Each of the numerous cities or city-states was located on the river or a canal. The porous, arid plain could be made productive only with elaborate irrigation systems to conserve and utilize the river-born moisture and nutrients. Scarce raw materials such as stone, timber, minerals, and metals had to come from trade but there was an abundance of material for bricks.

From the walled cities such as Uruk, Umma, and Lagash, urbanism spread north to Nineveh, east to Susa and farther afield to Mari and Ebla to the northwest. The riches of Mesopotamia often proved tempting and accessible to Sumer's neighbors from the north and east. The barbarian Guti, the Akkadians, Babylonians, and Assyrians all built on the Sumerian base. The technological, political, social, and economic foundations established in Sumer were carried to the colonies and palace cities to the north and west and parallel the developments in the Indus and Nile valleys as well.

It was in the second millennium B.C. that a new power from central Anatolia, the Hittites, entered the competitive arena. From their capital at Hattusas in the high plateau to the north, these aggressive invaders first challenged the Mitanni in northern Mesopotamia and eventually the Egyptian New Kingdom in the Levant. Down through the fourteenth and thirteenth centuries territorial expansion and especially Levantine maritime commerce were the prizes in this great international struggle. At the same time that the Hittites were looking to their west, the Mitanni were troubled by unrest from Ashur and the Egyptians were expanding to their south into Nubia with its attractive gold deposits.

EXERCISE 3
THE BEGINNINGS OF CIVILIZATION IN THE ANCIENT NEAR EAST: CITY-STATES AND INTERNATIONAL EMPIRES

I.   MAKING THE MAP

1.   Locate and label Mesopotamia, Sumer, Akkad, Babylonia, Elam, Assyria.
2.   Locate and label the Tigris River, Euphrates River, the Red Sea, and the Persian Gulf, Mediterranean Sea, the Halys River.
3.   Locate and label the Taurus Mountains, the Zagros Mountains, the Caucasus Mountains.
4.   Locate with a black dot and label Eridu, Uruk, Lagash, Ur, Umma, Mari Ebla, Agade, Babylon, Hattushas, Catalhüyük, Jarmo.
5.   Color in the area of the Hittite Empire *ca.* 1500 B.C.
6.   Show in different colors the approximate area of the Akkadian and Babylonian empires under Sargon and Hammurabi.

II.   READING THE MAP

1.   What is the direction of flow of the Tigris and Euphrates rivers?
2.   Into what body of water do these rivers flow?
3.   Mesopotamia is flanked by the Zagros Mountains on the _____ and by the Arabian Desert on the _____.
4.   Sargon of Akkad's empire stretched from the _____ Gulf on the south, north, and west to the shores of the _____ Sea.
5.   What is the approximate distance in miles from Uruk to Babylon?

III.   UNDERSTANDING THE MAP

1.   What was the source of wealth and power in the city-states of ancient Sumer?
2.   What was the likely reason for Hammurabi to install his capital at Babylon?
3.   What is the approximate distance in miles from Ur to Mari on the Euphrates?
4.   How would you describe the climate of Mesopotamia in terms of temperature and rainfall?
5.   Is Mesopotamia north or south of the Equator?
6.   From what regions did the invaders of Sumer originate?
7.   In what area was there territorial conflict between the Egyptian and Hittite empires in the fourteenth and thirteenth centuries B.C.?

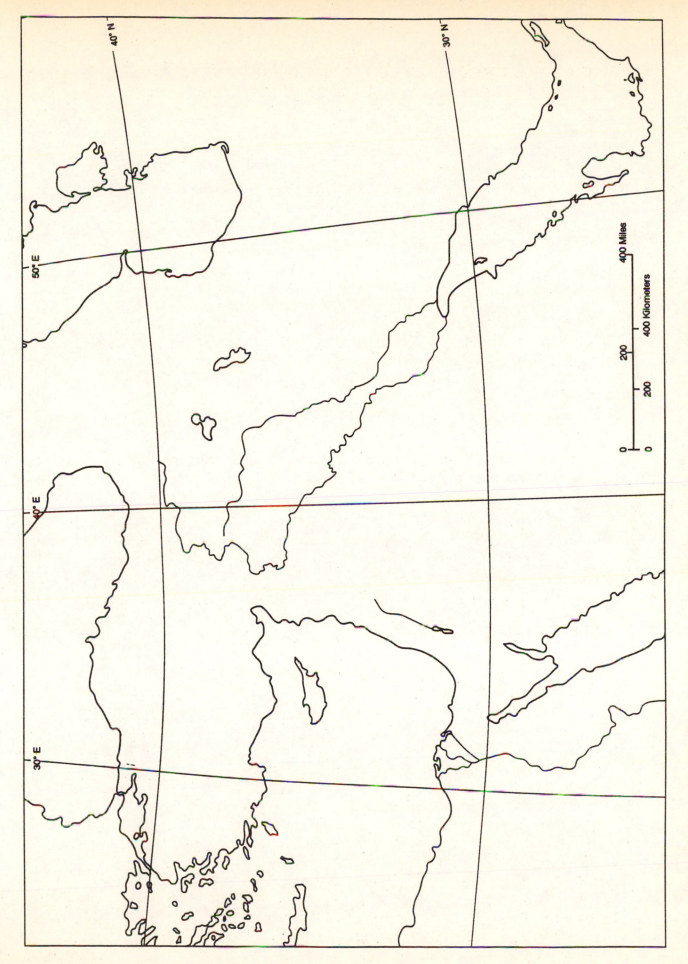

Exercise 3: The Beginnings of Civilization in the Ancient Near East: City States and International Empires

IV. EARLY CIVILIZATION IN ANCIENT EGYPT

Egyptian tradition credits Menes or Narmer with unifying Egypt in 3100 B.C. Political unity and technological advances made Egypt one of the richest, most powerful, and enduring states of the ancient Near East. In a region of sparse rainfall, the Nile River was the crucial element for survival and agricultural development. The course of the Nile takes it over four thousand miles flowing from modern Burundi in Central Africa northward to empty into the Mediterranean Sea. In its long trip the river flows from dense forests through barren, stony terrain descending over numerous cataracts or rapids to the desert floor. The distance from the first cataract to Lower Egypt or the Delta is nearly seven hundred miles. At the apex of the Delta the Nile divides into several branches. The Delta measures over nine thousand square miles in area—more than double the surface area of the fertile Upper Nile area, which is confined to the very narrow strip along both sides of the river.

The navigability of the Nile from the Delta to the first cataract made it a transportation and communication artery that contributed to Egypt's economic and political unity. The Nile was a continually renewable source of moisture and silt which created a narrow but very rich belt of fertile land. Throughout antiquity, its unique combination of climate and topography made Egypt a proverbial breadbasket. The predictable stable flow of the Nile enhanced by the technology of basin and irrigation systems contributed to Egypt's sense of confidence, security, and longevity. In addition to the valley's agricultural wealth, game and essential salt were drawn from the Delta, while stone and minerals were to be found in abundance upriver. Egypt's isolated position—flanked by deserts on the west and east, mountains and forests to the south, and the Mediterranean Sea to the north—strengthened the sense of security and divine support.

About ten thousand years ago, post-glacial changes in the region's climate contributed to the development of hunting-gathering and semi-nomadic groups. By the seventh millennium small agricultural villages emerged in the Delta and Lower Nile Valley. Technological advances, prosperity, and population growth contributed to political organizations called *nomes*. Major administrative centers were located at Buto in Lower Egypt and at Hierakonopolis in Upper Egypt. Under the patriarchal and divinely mandated pharaonic monarchy established by Menes, Memphis became the capital of a unified kingdom. The exploitation of Egypt's resources never required the heavy concentration of population in urban centers (as in Sumer) and much of the rural character of the land persisted.

For hundreds of years during the Old Kingdom, the potential of Egypt was realized for the glory of the god/kings and the material benefit of their loyal subjects. The construction of royal administrative, religious, and funerary centers at Sakkara and Giza matched and even exceeded the technological achievements of hydraulic engineering applied to the Nile.

The wealth and tranquility of the Old Kingdom were finally shattered in the twenty-second century B.C. by difficulties perhaps aggravated by successive periods of insufficient inundations. A second shock struck the kingdom in the eighteenth century B.C. when western Asian warrior migrants breached the frontiers and established themselves in the Northeast Delta. In the period known as the New Kingdom or Empire, Egypt acquired foreign territory for the first time (except for Nubia) by advancing into Syria and Palestine to compete in the international arena with the Hittite Empire. Subsequently they would be forced to defend themselves against the "Peoples of the Sea" and accommodate to a Libyan occupation before succumbing successively to Ethiopians, Nubians, Persians, and Greeks.

EXERCISE 4
EARLY CIVILIZATION IN ANCIENT EGYPT

I.   MAKING THE MAP (Two Maps)

1.   Locate and label the Nile River, the Mediterranean Sea, the Gulf of Suez, the Red Sea.
2.   Locate and label the Nile Delta, Upper Egypt.
3.   Locate and label the Sahara Desert, the Sinai Peninsula.
4.   Locate with a black dot and label Thebes, Memphis, Giza, Saggarah, Akenaten (Amarna), Elephantine, Abu Simbel, Kadesh, Karnak.
5.   Locate and label Palestine, Syria, Cyprus, Crete, Anatolia, Mesopotamia.
6.   Color in the area of the Hittite Empire and the Empire of Egypt about 1350 B.C.

II.   READING THE MAP

1.   What is the area of origin and direction of flow of the Nile River?
2.   Into what body of water does the Nile empty?
3.   What is the average width, in miles, of ancient Egypt from the Delta to Elephantine?
4.   A route due east from Memphis along the thirtieth parallel would take you to what city in ancient Sumer?
5.   What is the name given to the land west of Egypt?
6.   What is the approximate distance in miles between Memphis and Thebes?

III.   UNDERSTANDING THE MAP

1.   What natural barriers protected Egypt during the Old and Middle Kingdoms?
2.   What are the cataracts of the Nile and where are they located?
3.   Who were the peoples who first breached Egypt's frontiers and what was their route?
4.   To what do the terms Upper and Lower Egypt refer?
5.   How would you describe the climate of Egypt?
6.   Approximately how far is Memphis in Egypt from the Equator?
7.   Compare the topography and climate of Upper and Lower Egypt.
8.   What is the name of the land from just east of Egypt and due north of the Red Sea?
9.   What was the major threat to Egypt under the New Kingdom and where was the main area of their conflict?

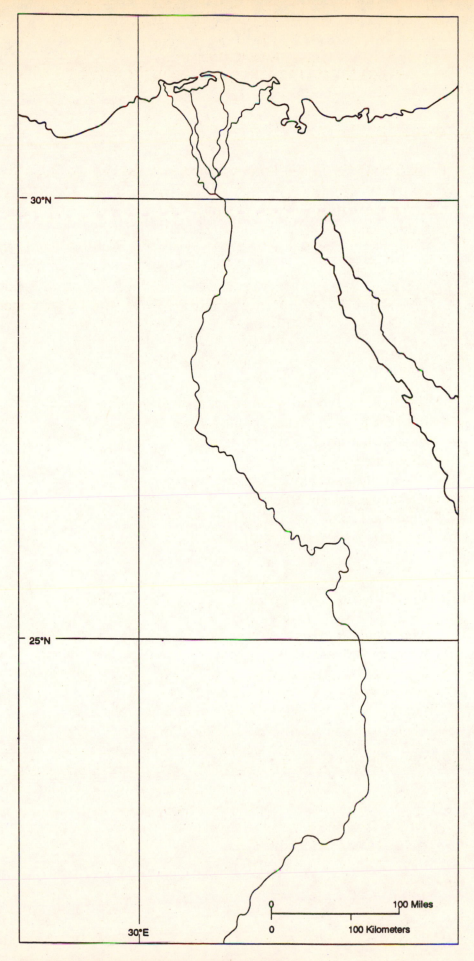

30°N

25°N

30°E

100 Miles

0   100 Kilometers

Exercise 4: Early Civilization in Ancient Egypt

17

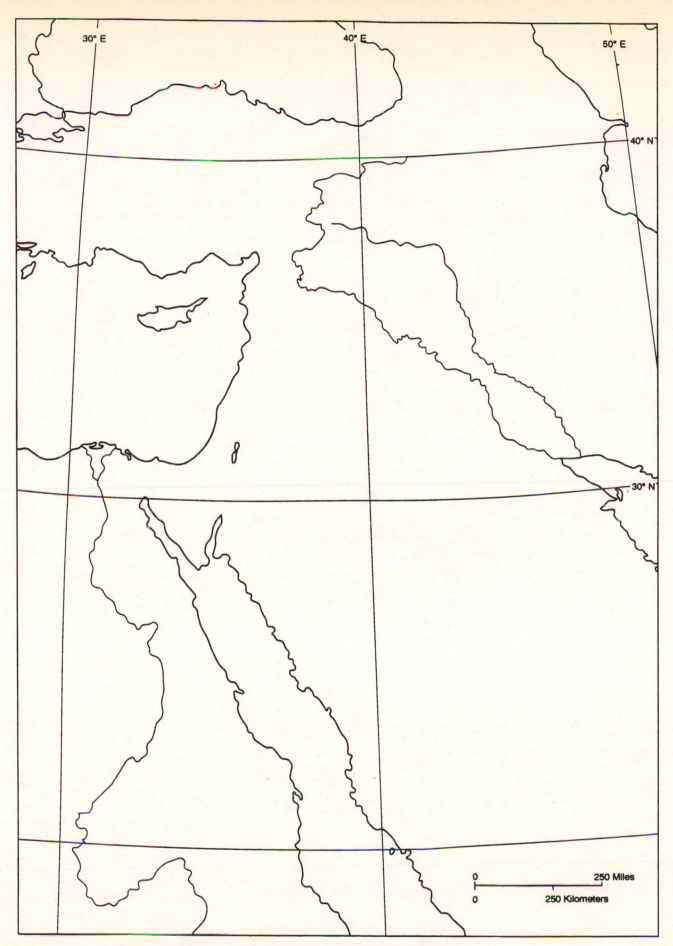

Israel, Judah, the Ancient Hebrews and their Neighbors

V. ISRAEL, JUDAH, THE ANCIENT HEBREWS, AND THEIR NEIGHBORS

The united kingdom of Israel and Judah, under David and Solomon, was realized in the tenth century B.C., only after hundreds of years of migration and hardship. The capital was established at Jerusalem. The Hebrews, Israelites, or Jews were related to the larger group of Semitic speakers known as the Aramaeans. Originally nomadic and pastoral, their traditions connected them with Ur in Sumer. From there fortune took them north toward Haran and to the southwest where some of their number came under Egyptian rule. The long and difficult trek out of Egypt across the Sinai, the making of the Covenant with their national God, and eventual settlement in Palestine (attributed to Moses) is likely a telescoping of a complex and lengthy process. The contacts with Midianites and the conflicts and compromises with the Canaanites over land and livelihood all had their impact.

The hardships of captivity, migration, and struggle for survival all tested, enriched, and strengthened the Hebrews' vision of themselves and their destiny. The transition from tribal nomadic traditions to sedentary agriculture and urban patterns brought additional challenges. This was not a particularly inviting area nor could it support the large population of an area such as Egypt or Sumer. The Jordan is the major source of fresh water. The salt lake called the Dead Sea is the lowest point on Earth: 1,296 feet below sea level.

Early Jericho had been an oasis-based settlement. This region, dominated by desert and mountains, suffers from limited rainfall and thin, poor soil. The Mediterranean shore to the west is not noted for good harbors. Phoenicia, to the north, with Sidon, Tyre, and Byblos, is the exception in that respect. The Philistine strongholds to the south were fortified city-states established by newcomers who may be associated with the "Peoples of the Sea." The meager resources resulted in much contentiousness among the would-be nationbuilders in the region. Furthermore, the area was a land of passage for north-south and east-west routes. Damascus, to the north, became an important focus in overland trade. The Phoenicians opened the Mediterranean sea lanes to create opportunities far beyond their limited local resources.

The Hebrew amalgam which culminated in the short-lived unified kingdom of Israel had the strategically located Jerusalem as its capital. Briefly it became a royal center for international diplomacy under Solomon and then David, who had been very resourceful in his struggles against Ammonites, Moabites, Edomites, and Philistines. Common origins and religious beliefs, which had bound the traditional twelve tribes, ultimately proved ineffective in the face of emerging competitive struggles. The united kingdom soon broke up as the result of severe internal trials.

Israel fell to the expansionist Assyrians in the eighth century and the capital, Samaria, was destroyed in 722 B.C. The Kingdom of Judah succumbed to the neo-Babylonians or Chaldeans in 587 B.C. The humiliation of dispersal and captivity of many Jews followed the destruction of Jerusalem. Cyrus II, The Great, creator of the new Persian Empire, restored Jerusalem and Judah's fortunes once more, after 539. Even after the conquest of Alexander the Great and Roman expansion in the region, Jerusalem remained, for some time, the political and spiritual center of the Jews. Judaism, the faith of the Hebrews, would, in fact, transcend the traditional concept of a territorial state and survive the Roman destruction of Jerusalem.

EXERCISE 5
ISRAEL, JUDAH, THE ANCIENT HEBREWS, AND THEIR NEIGHBORS .

I.   MAKING THE MAP

1.   Locate and label Syria, Palestine, Egypt, Mesopotamia, Babylonia, Assyria, Chaldea, Phoenicia, Philistia, the Sinai Peninsula.
2.   Locate and label the Mediterranean Sea, the Dead Sea, the Red Sea, Sea of Galilee, the Jordan River, the Nile River.
3.   Locate with a black dot and label Shiloh, Aphek, Jerusalem, Shechem, Byblos, Tyre, Sidon, Babylon, Nineveh, Jericho, Samaria, Damascus.
4.   Show in different colors the area of Judah and Israel.

II.   READING THE MAP

1.   What body of water flanks the western side of the Kingdom of Israel?
2.   What is the approximate distance from Jerusalem to Babylon?
3.   What is the approximate area in square miles of the United Kingdom of Israel under King Solomon?
4.   What were the neighboring states located to the east of ancient Israel?
5.   What is the approximate distance in miles between Memphis and Jerusalem?

III.   UNDERSTANDING THE MAP

1.   How would you account in historical terms for the growth of the Kingdom of Israel under David and Solomon?
2.   Against what groups did the early Hebrews compete for territory?
3.   To what powerful neighbors did the Kingdom of Israel eventually fall?
4.   Israel's active neighbor to the northwest responded to expansionist states in a different way. Name that state and its alternative to conquest and submission.
5.   To what ancient city did the Hebrews trace their origins under the patriarch Abraham?

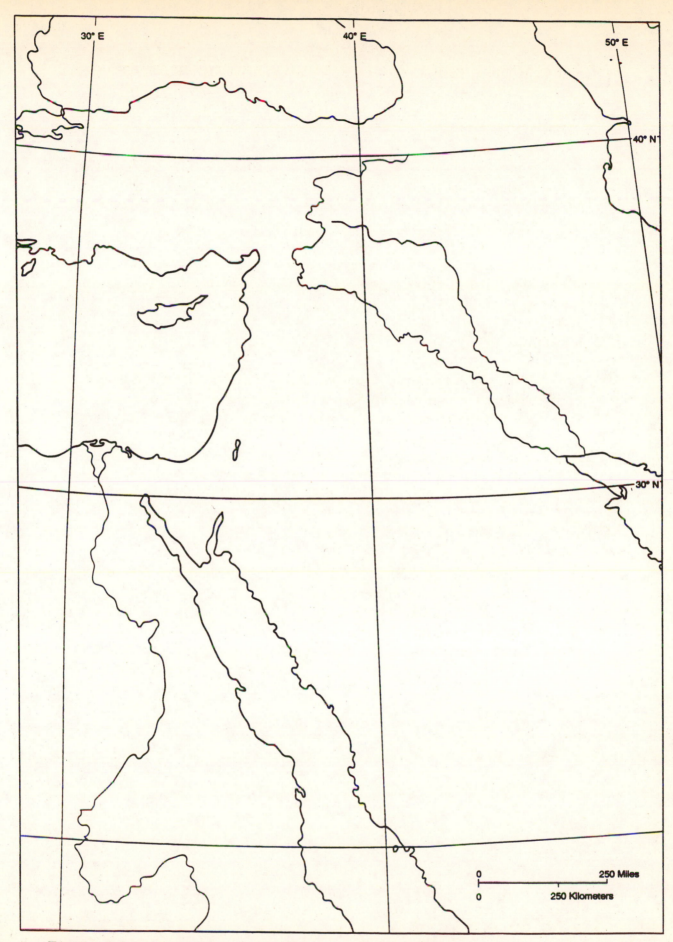

Exercise 5: Israel, Judah, the Ancient Hebrews and their Neighbors

VI. THE AGE OF EMPIRES: BABYLONIA , ASSYRIA , PERSIA

The territorial ambitions of the Akkadians under Sargon the Great and Narim Sin in the twenty-fourth and twenty-third centuries B.C. were taken up by the vigorous Amorites under Hammurabi in the eighth century B.C. Babylon, on the Euphrates, became the capital of this powerful southern Mesopotamian kingdom. Hammurabi's successors were unable to stave off the invasion of the Kassites in the sixteenth century B.C., but Babylon recovered under Nebuchadnezzar I in the twelfth century B.C. and more significantly under his namesake in the sixth century in what is called the Neo-Babylonian or Chaldean Empire. Babylon remained a great cultural center, preserving the Sumerian-Akkadian cultural legacy despite the Hittite destruction, the Kassite and Assyrian occupations, and Persian conquest under Cyrus the Great.

The centuries-long struggle of the Assyrians, who were first centered in the agriculturally rich area of the northern Tigris River at Ashur, resulted in a ruthlessly powerful empire. It eventually included all of Mesopotamia, Syria, Palestine, and for a time, even Egypt. Only Urartu, farther to the north, resisted their incursions. The Assyrians were tested and toughened for generations in their struggle with the likes of the Hittites, Hurrians, and the Mitanni. The Assyrian agricultural economy was supplemented by the importation of horses, metals, and timber from their neighbors in the mountainous areas to their east. Under Tiglath-pileser III in the eighth century a thousand-year effort produced a large-scale empire. This empire was built by dynamic leaders who employed a highly refined military machine and terror tactics. The Assyrian Empire was administered in succession from Ashur, Nimrud, Khorsabad, and finally at Nineveh. It was, in fact, ultimately overstretched beyond its resources and lacked the vital element of consensus.

Under Cyrus II, the Great, the Achaemenid Persians surpassed their one-time allies, the Medes, to build the Near East's largest and most efficient empire. Their ancestors were Indo-European speakers originally from central Asia. They settled on the Iranian plateau between Mesopotamia and India to the east. The Lydian Kingdom and Ionian Greek cities in Western Anatolia and Babylonia soon fell to Cyrus. Egypt, too, along with Syria and Palestine, were brought into the Persian orbit. To the east the areas up to the Indus River were incorporated into the empire by the end of the sixth century, under Darius. Persian attempts to penetrate Europe beyond the Bosphorus were less successful in the long run, and the Greek city-states frustrated further expansion there in the fifth century under Xerxes.

Administrative organization, leadership, and a national will to power created and held the Persian Empire together, The kings operated out of their capitals of Susa, Ecbatana, Persepolis, Babylon, Sardis, and Pasargadae. The twenty satrapies or provinces were linked by a network of royal roads which made for efficient communication and military movement. Maritime traffic moved through a Persian-developed canal between the Nile River and the Red Sea. Phoenician fleets were utilized in the eastern Mediterranean Sea. This largest of empires tolerated a measure of ethnic and national diversity in return for obedience, financial tribute, and military conscription. The Persian Empire was, however, threatened by nomadic incursions on its northwest frontier, suffered humiliation at the hands of the numerically weaker Greeks, and was destined to be plagued by internal dynastic problems until overrun by an even more ambitious empire-builder, Alexander the Great of Macedon.

EXERCISE 6
THE AGE OF EMPIRES: BABYLONIA, ASSYRIA, PERSIA

I.   MAKING THE MAP

1.   Locate and label the Tigris River, the Euphrates River, the Aegean Sea, the Persian Gulf, the Mediterranean Sea, the Black Sea, the Red Sea, the Nile River, the Indus River, the Caspian Sea.
2.   Locate with a black dot and label Ninevah, Babylon, Memphis, Susa, Ecbatana, Persepolis, Sardis, Jerusalem, Damascus.
3.   Color in blue the area of the Assyrian Empire at its peak under Esar-Haddon.
4.   Color in red the area of the Neo-Babylonian Empire under Nebuchadnezzar II.
5.   Color in yellow the area of the Persian Empire under Darius I.
6.   Locate and label Lydia, Ionia, Media, Egypt.

II.   READING THE MAP

1.   The approximate distance in miles from Nineveh to Babylon is _____ .
2.   Name the mountain chain to the east of the Tigris River.
3.   Name the states which fell under Assyrian rule at its peak of power.
4.   What is the approximate size in square miles of the Neo-Babylonian Empire?
5.   What is the approximate distance in miles from Persepolis to Sardis?
6.   What major states were incorporated into the Persian Empire?
7.   Where did Persian expansion meet major resistance and defeat in the early fifth century B.C.?

III.   UNDERSTANDING THE MAP

1.   What do you think enabled the Assyrians and Persians to conquer and administer such vast empires?
2.   What was the fate of Egypt in the conflict with Persia?
3.   How did Israel fare under the Assyrians, Neo-Babylonians, and Persians?
4.   What major river system formed the eastern limits of the Persian Empire?

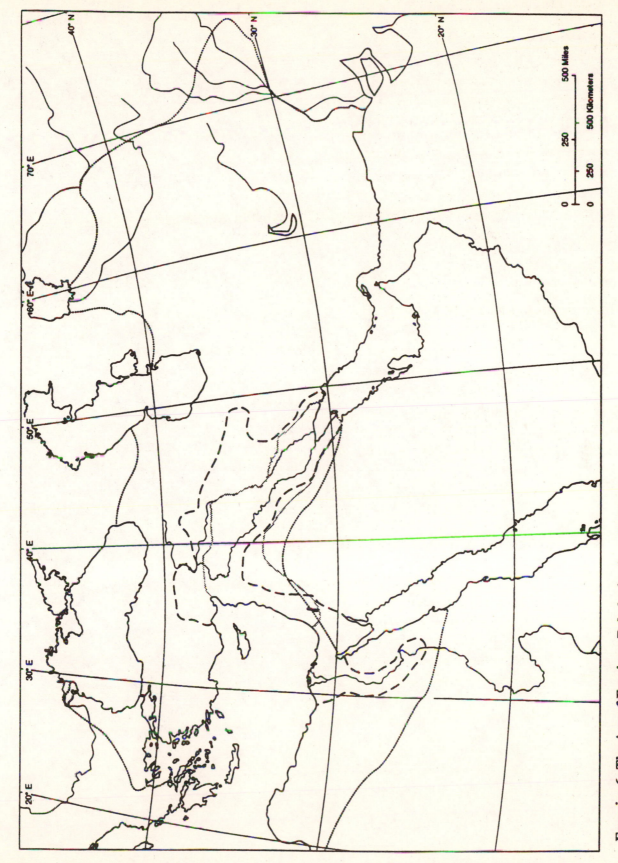

Exercise 6: The Age of Empires: Babylonia, Assyria, Persia

500 Miles

0   250   500 Kilometers

VII. EARLY CIVILIZATION IN INDIA

The most important early civilization in the Indian subcontinent developed by about 3000 B.C. Neolithic centers on the Indus River, such as those at Amri, Kulli, Nundara, and Nal, anticipate the developments at Harappa. A number of rivers flow southwest between the Thar Desert and Baluchistan to the west. This river system originates 1,800 miles distant in the Himalaya Mountains and eventually empties into the Arabian Sea. The annual inundations deposited rich silt but could also obliterate settlements with uncontrolled destructive flooding.

Mohenjo Daro and Harappa were two of the most important complex urban centers. They were located some three hundred miles and seven hundred miles respectively upriver. These and other sites were the focus of productive agricultural communities which grew wheat, barley and cotton. Their technology included tools of stone, copper, and bronze. Manufacture and trade supplemented the economy. In addition to riverine commerce there were overseas trade relations westward to the Persian Gulf and Mesopotamia. Overland trade extended far afield to Persia and Afghanistan.

These cities, which may have had populations of up to thirty-five thousand, were laid out in a systematic grid pattern, complete with granaries and drainage systems. The main construction material was fired brick, which may have contributed in the long run to deforestation as fuel for the kilns was extracted. Fortified citadels were an essential element in the makeup of each community. From the evidence available, it is not clear whether Harappa and Mohenjo Daro were dual capitals of a unified state or administrative centers of individual political units. In any case, Harappa and Mohenjo Daro were two core cities among many in a civilization covering perhaps five hundred thousand square miles in the Indus Valley extending south to the Narbada and to the north at Rupar.

Harappan civilization existed for about one thousand years. It may have been natural causes, human activity, or some combination that contributed to a decline beginning about 2000 B.C. It has been suggested that a shift in the course of the Indus, a breakdown of the irrigation technology, and civil strife may have been negative factors in the equation. Deforestation and the collapse of the complex trade network have been proposed as further complications.

The decline and fall of the Early Indian civilization may have anticipated the appearance of Aryan newcomers *ca*. 1500 B.C. These invaders were a branch of other Indo-European language groups and they appeared in the northwest regions of India. From the literature of their culture they are often referred to as the Rig-veda or Veda Aryans. After their initial phase of entry (some five hundred years) in the Late Vedic Era, they expanded eastward to the Ganges River area. This river system originates in the Himalayas, over fifteen hundred miles away, and flows into the Bay of Bengal near modern Calcutta. Originally pastoral/hunters, the Aryans came to utilize horses and fast chariots to conquer and dominate a territory that would stretch from the Bay of Bengal west to the Persian Gulf. It included lands from the Himalaya Mountains in the north, beyond the Vindhya Range, south to the Godavari River. These people eventually cleared the forests and converted much of northern India to agriculture, exploiting the labor of the subjugated population. The north-south geographic dividing line is the Vindhya Range and the Narbada River.

EXERCISE 7
EARLY CIVILIZATION IN INDIA

I.   MAKING THE MAP

1.   Locate and label the Himalaya Mountains, the Hindu Kush, the Vindhya Range, the Deccan Plateau, the Tibetan Plateau, the Thar Desert, the Kirthar Range, the Western Ghats.
2.   Locate and label the Indus River, the Ganges River, the Brahmaputra River, the Godavari River, the Narbada (Narmada) River.
3.   Locate and label the Arabian Sea, the Bay of Bengal.
4.   Locate with a black dot and label Harappa, Mohenjo Daro.
5.   Locate and label Baluchistan, Hindustan, Punjab, Tamil Land, Sri Lanka, Nepal.

II.   READING THE MAP

1.   The Indian subcontinent covers approximately _____ square miles.
2.   India is flanked by the _____ Sea and the Bay of _____ to the east.
3.   The earliest civilization in India developed in the area of the _____ River.
4.   The Aryans invaded India from the _____ and settled in the area of the _____ River.
5.   In general, India could be divided into two regions: the _____ of the north, and the _____ of the south.

III.   UNDERSTANDING THE MAP

1.   What factors of the natural setting contributed to the development of the earliest civilizations in India?
2.   What barriers limited contacts between India and the regions to the northeast?
3.   What is the dominant feature of the area of India to the south and east of the Indus River Valley?

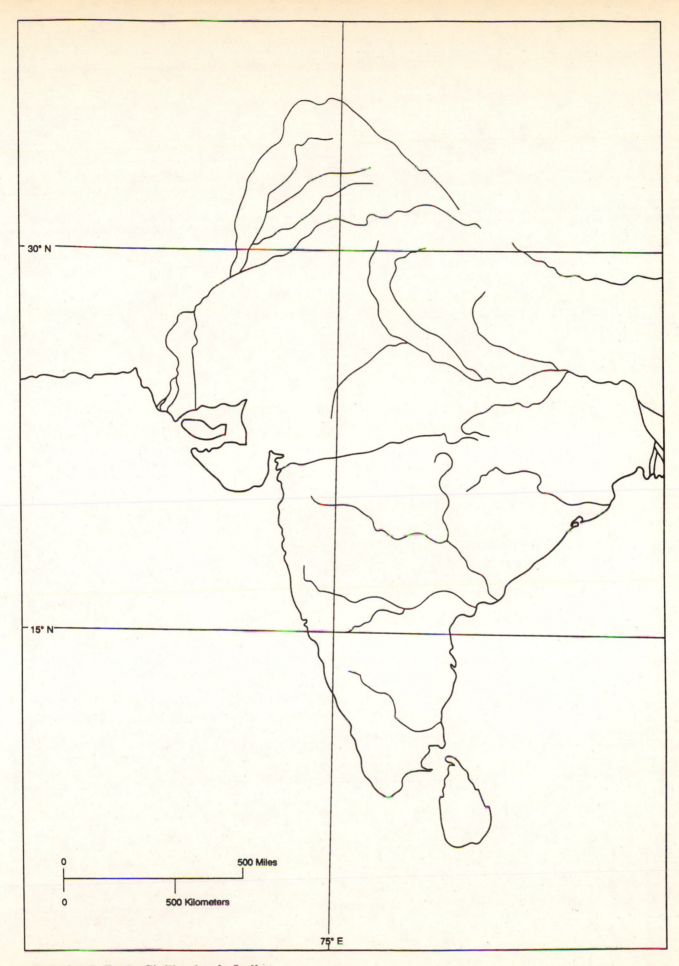

Exercise 7: Early Civilization in India

VIII. EARLY CHINA

The huge nation of China is today the largest in the Far East. It is, in fact, slightly larger in surface area than the United States. The population, nearly one and one-quarter billion, is the largest of any nation on Earth. However, only twelve percent of China's land is suitable for agriculture (compared to twenty-three percent of the United States). The Yangtze (Yongzi) River is one of the world's largest systems, extending nearly four thousand miles from its origins on the Tibetan Plateau to the East China Sea. The Yellow (Huang Ho) River meanders widely across northern China before emptying into the Gulf of Chihli. The vast expanse of China has long been isolated by a variety of terrain including mountains and deserts to the northwest, west, and southwest. The steppes of Central Asia pose another extended formidable barrier between the lands of China and the West. To the north lie the equally forbidding regions of Siberia, Mongolia, and Manchuria. To the east the East China Sea and the South China Sea lead into the world's largest ocean, the Pacific. Climate zones range from the subtropical to the subarctic.

Compared to some regions, China is well watered from rain and its rivers. It has been, however, continually subject to natural catastrophes such as floods, droughts, famines, and earthquakes. Geographic and topographic factors have contributed to a generally isolated independent path to civilization. The Chinese would eventually have a considerable role in Japan, Korea, and Vietnam to the east.

In the long Paleolithic era hominids appeared in the area of Kwangsi, Yunnan and Shansi. About 500,000 B.C. Peking man appeared in the north. Remains of *Homo sapiens* dating to 30,000 B.C. have been found in the Ordos Desert region as well as in areas to the southwest. Neolithic agricultural communities emerged in three areas in the eighth and seventh millennia: the highland plains of the Yellow (Huang Ho) River, the lower Yangtze (Yongzi) and Huai Rivers, and the coastal areas of the southeast.

It was the easily worked wind-deposited *loess* soil of the Yellow River Valley that was particularly suitable to agricultural development. Irrigation and drainage technology boosted the productive capacities for wheat and millet. Rice was introduced from the southeast as early as 5,000 B.C.

Early stages in the beginnings of civilization are clearly indicated in the distinctive pottery styles of Yangshao and Longshan. A true Bronze Age culture appeared with the historic Shang dynasty perhaps as early as the eighth century. Historical evidence for the preceding legendary Hsia (Xia), *ca*. 2000 B.C. is at present very limited. The two-horse war chariot, perhaps imported through Western contacts, was a major instrument of Shang expansion and control. A system of writing and bronze-working technology were other important advances in this era. Many towns grew into true cities in the Shang period. These cities served as royal residences, administrative and religious centers, and some covered an area as large as ten square miles.

Monumental architecture and extensive fortifications were characteristic features of such sites as Loyang, Chengchou, and Anyang. The labor force appears to have included large numbers of slaves. Rich royal graves testify to the military might and wide-ranging luxury trade dominated by dynastic leaders. Internal unrest and rebellious vassals from the Wei River Valley to the west eventually destroyed the Shang capital at Anyang in the mid eleventh century.

EXERCISE 8
EARLY CHINA

I.   MAKING THE MAP

1.   Locate and label the Gobi Desert, the Yellow River, the Yangtze River, the Wei River, the Yellow Sea, the East China Sea.
2.   Locate and label Mongolia, Taiwan, Korea, Tibet, the Shantung (Shandong) Peninsula, the Szechuan (Sichuan) Basin.
3.   Locate with a black dot and label Anyang, Loyang, Chengchou (Zengzhou).
4.   Color in red the area of the Shang Kingdom.
5.   Color in blue the area of the Western Chou (Zhou) Kingdom.

II.   READING THE MAP

1.   The Yangtze River flows roughly _____ to _____ and empties into the _____ Sea.
2.   China today is bordered on the north by _____ and _____.
3.   The large peninsula to the northeast of China is called _____ today.
4.   The large island directly off the southeast coast of China is called _____ today.
5.   The area encompassed by the Chang Kingdom was approximately _____ square miles.

III.   UNDERSTANDING THE MAP

1.   In what regions did civilization begin in early China?
2.   What were some of the agricultural methods and products in these regions?
3.   What are the major characteristics of the Yellow River which play a part in the successful practice of agriculture?
4.   What is the predominant feature of the landscape of northwest China?
5.   A line drawn due east around the globe from Harbin in north China would put a traveller into what area of North America?
6.   A line drawn due east around the globe from Hong Kong in South China would put one in the capital of what Latin American nation?

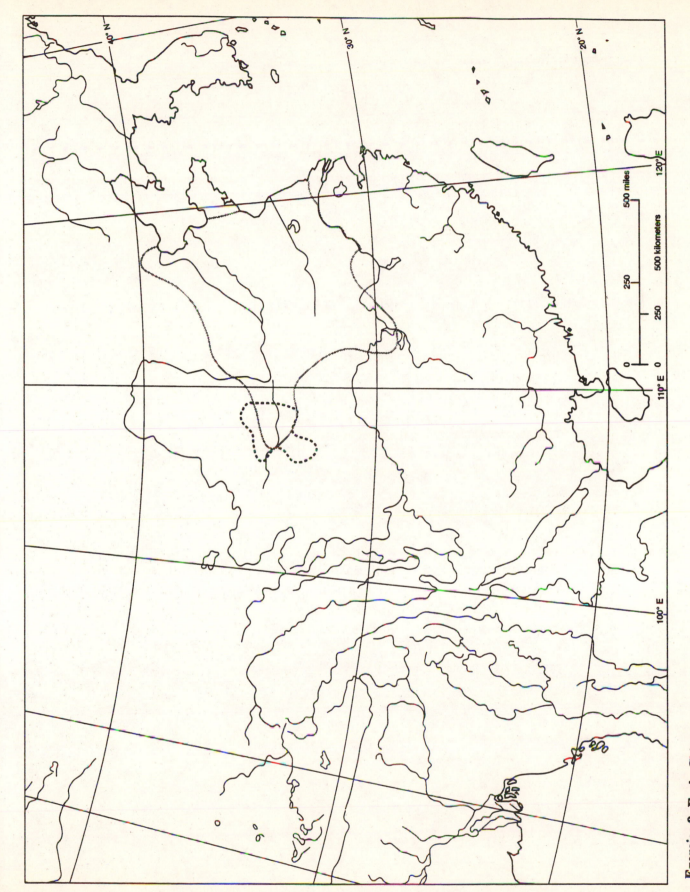

Exercise 8: Early China

500 miles

500 kilometers

IX. EARLY CIVILIZATION IN MIDDLE AND SOUTH AMERICA

The Americas are made up of North, Middle (or Central), and South America. North America is about four thousand miles wide in the north and only thirty-one miles wide at the isthmus which connects it with South America. The continents are separated from Europe and Africa by the Atlantic Ocean and from Asia by the Pacific Ocean. North and Middle America, with a total of twelve million square miles, have twenty-three countries today. There are twelve countries in the ten million square miles of South America. North America is the third largest continent on Earth and Canada is the second largest nation. Brazil, to the south, is the world's fifth largest nation. The Amazon River is nearly twice as long as the Mississippi. Our five Great Lakes, located between Canada and the United States, comprise the largest body of fresh water in the world. Climate regions and topography in these continents range from the Arctic to the tropical and from rain forest (Brazil's is the largest in the world), plains, woodlands, and deserts to rugged mountains. The highest peak is Mount Aconcagua in Argentina. At 22,834 feet it is second only to Mount Everest and higher than Mount McKinley in Alaska. From Chile north to Alaska there are fifty active volcanoes.

The most recent evidence confirms that human beings found their way into the Americas at least as early as thirty thousand years ago. Nomadic hunter-gatherers from Asia crossed the land bridge, which emerged at the Bering Strait, in several waves during the growth and recession of glaciers. Nomadic hunters in pursuit of bigger game made the trip from Siberia to Alaska and beyond into the game lands which emerged as the glaciers receded after 12,000 B.C. The descendants of the newcomers eventually made their way as far as the tip of South America and eastward to the Atlantic shore and in the process hunted much of the early large game to extinction. The great bison, three varieties of mammoths, the ground sloth, camels, the early horse, and many other animals were exterminated. Climate change, the decline in available food, and population increases may have been contributory factors as well.

The ensuing struggle for survival varied from the hunters and fishers of the Arctic regions to the coastal and river fishers and woodland hunter-gatherers in North America. As early as 5000 B.C. some communities developed simple agricultural techniques. In the plateau of central Mexico, the lowland areas of the Gulf of Mexico and in the central Andes, corn (maize), beans, potatoes, peanuts and other nutritious plant foods were cultivated. The cultivation of corn eventually spread to the southwest and northeast of North America. Climate, moisture, the length of the growing season, and human ingenuity would determine the limits of these indigenous technological developments.

Early advances culminated in large-scale urban-administrative-ritual centers, paralleling those in Mesopotamia or Egypt, but apparently in isolation. Monumental architecture, water control systems, basic metallurgy, and complex commercial patterns contributed to the greatness of these civilizations. An advanced script, significant developments in astronomy, and mathematics demonstrate the high level of achievements of the Maya. True states with diverse populations in the thousands emerged in the Olmec of the Gulf coast, the Zapotecs in the Oaxaca Valley, and at Teotihuacan in central Mexico. The Maya in Guatemala and the Chavín and Huari in the Andes are additional examples of early civilizations. At its peak, Teotihuacan in Mexico could boast a population of over 125,000 in its twelve square miles of territory. It was but one variation of political and economic systems stretching from the Adena and Hopewell to Chavín and Huari.

EXERCISE 9
EARLY CIVILIZATION IN MIDDLE AND SOUTH AMERICA

I. **MAKING THE MAP**

1. Locate and label Central America, South America, the Pacific Ocean, the Atlantic Ocean, the Gulf of Mexico, the Caribbean Sea, Lake Titicaca.
2. Draw the line of the Equator, the Tropic of Cancer and the Tropic of Capricorn.
3. Locate and label the Andes Mountains, the Yucatan Peninsula, the Amazon River, the Valley of Mexico, the Sierra Madre Mountains.
4. Locate with a black dot and label San Lorenzo, La Venta, Tres Zapotes, Teotihuacan, Tikal, El Mirador, Chitzén Itzá, Tihuananco, Tula, Huari.
5. Color in green the area of the Olmec Territory.
6. Color in red the areas controlled by the Maya.

II. **READING THE MAP**

1. The earliest civilization in Middle America developed in what is now _____, _____, and _____.
2. In South America the earliest center of civilization originated in the _____ Mountains in the modern states of _____, _____, and _____.
3. Lake Titicaca, in what is now _____, was the site of the important city of _____ in the fourteenth century B.C.
4. The Olmec civilization in Middle America originated in the area of _____ and _____.

III. **UNDERSTANDING THE MAP**

1. Describe the topographical features of the areas in which civilization began in South America.
2. What terms would best describe the climate of the area where the Olmec civilization began?
3. What methods were developed to practice productive agriculture in the area of Yucatan, Guatemala, and Belize in the Maya territories?

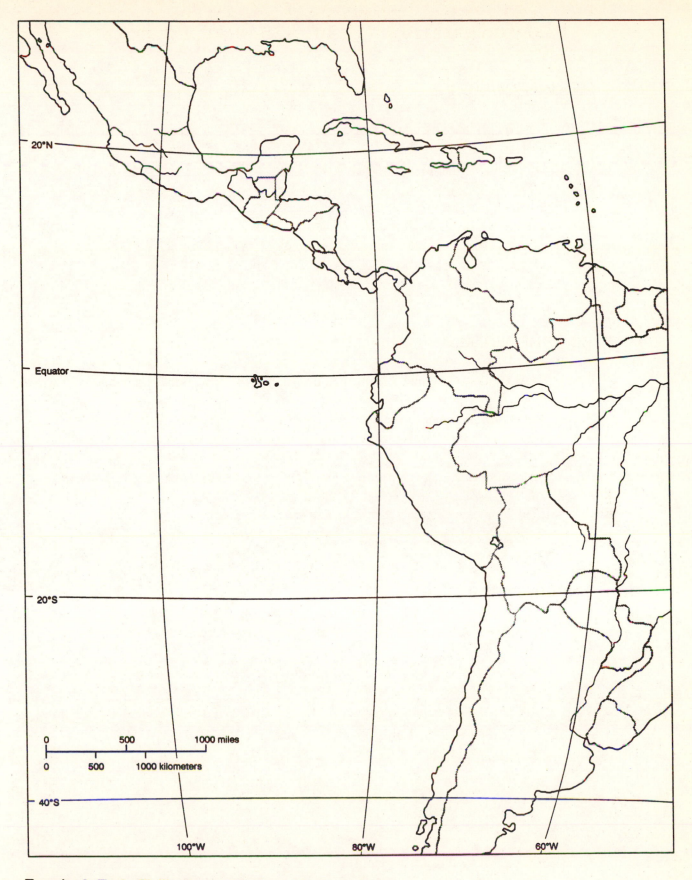

20°N

Equator

20°S

| 0 | 500 | 1000 miles |
| 0 | 500 | 1000 kilometers |

40°S

100°W   80°W   60°W

Exercise 9: Early Civilization in Middle and South America

X. THE EARLY AEGEAN

The Greek Peninsula is located at the extreme southeastern edge of Europe. It is separated from Asia Minor (Anatolia) to the east by the Aegean Sea. It is barely fifty miles across the Ionian Sea from the island of Corfu west to southern Italy. The route to the Black Sea (Euxine), to the northeast, is through the Hellespont (Dardanelles), the Sea of Marmara, and the Bosphorus. The Aegean Sea is dotted with two thousand islands, of which less than 170 are habitable for lack of fresh water. The Cyclades Islands are an extension of the southeast mainland and include Paros, Naxos, Melos, Thera, and Delos. The Sporades Islands hug the Anatolian coast and include Samos and Rhodes. The long narrow island of Crete lies to the south of the Aegean.

The mainland of Greece is actually quite small in surface area. From Mount Olympus, in the north, it is scarcely two hundred miles to the tip of Laconia in the south. The distance from Achaea, in the west, to the shore of Attica in the east is one hundred and fifty miles. The amount of arable land is limited to less than twenty-five percent of the total. The soil in the few areas of plains is generally poor and not well watered. The most conspicuous topographical features of the region are mountains and the sea. The Pindus and Parnon are the dominant north-south ranges. Central Greece and the Ionian regions of Anatolia are, however, blessed with fine natural harbors. The many islands make for relatively easy two-way communication across the Aegean.

As early as 6000 B.C., early agricultural settlements appeared in northeast Thessaly, Central Greece and on Crete. Migrants established the flourishing settlements of Dhimini, Sesklo, and others in Attica. Crete took the lead when Bronze Age technology came to the region. Knossos, Phaestos, Gournia, Mallia, in the northern and eastern sections of the island, are among the important centers. Minoan civilization would be the major power in the Aegean until the fifteenth century. This rich civilization had important cultural and commercial relations with Cyprus, Mesopotamia, Asia Minor and Egypt. The Cyclades Islands were home to distinctive and parallel developments in the same period.

A new element entered the picture perhaps as early as 2000 B.C. Pastoral-warriors related to other Indo-European language groups forced their way into the mainland and beyond. These newcomers established themselves in fortified citadels such as Mycenae, Tiryns, Thebes, Athens, Gla, and others. These early Greeks eventually moved beyond their initial cultural and technical achievements to dominate the Minoans and become the most powerful element in the Aegean by the fifteenth century. Massively fortified palace administrative centers and monumental architecture testify to their wealth and power. Legend and the poems of Homer associate them with the great war with the strategically located Troy in Asia Minor. In the twelfth century the Mycenaean system and the Aegean area began to enter the Dark Age after a period of widespread catastrophic disturbances.

EXERCISE 10
THE EARLY AEGEAN

I.   MAKING THE MAP

1.   Locate and label the Mediterranean Sea, the Ionian Sea, the Aegean Sea, the Black Sea, the Adriatic Sea, the Gulf of Corinth, the Hellespont, the Bosphorus.
2.   Locate and label Asia Minor, the Peloponnesus, Thrace, Thessaly, Attica.
3.   Locate and label the Cyclades Islands, Crete, Rhodes, Naxos, Thera, Euboea, Ithaca.
4.   Locate with a black dot and label Knossos, Phaestos, Mycenae, Tiryns, Pylos, Athens, Sparta, Thebes, Corinth, Troy.

II.   READING THE MAP

1.   The island of Crete is located approximately _____ miles from mainland Greece.
2.   The Greek Peninsula covers approximately _____ square miles.
3.   The largest island in the Aegean Sea is _____, located just east of _____.
4.   At the closest point, Europe and Asia Minor are separated by what body of water?
5.   Crete is located approximately _____ miles from Egypt.
6.   The Peloponnesus is connected to central Greece by the _____.

III.   UNDERSTANDING THE MAP

1.   By what means and from what general directions is it assumed that Bronze Age invaders entered Greece?
2.   In what areas did Dorians settle in the period following the end of the Bronze Age in Greece?
3.   What areas to the south and east had significant cultural and economic importance for Crete?
4.   Speculate on the possible importance of the location of Troy in the late Bronze Age.
5.   What do you consider the most significant elements of the topography of mainland Greece?

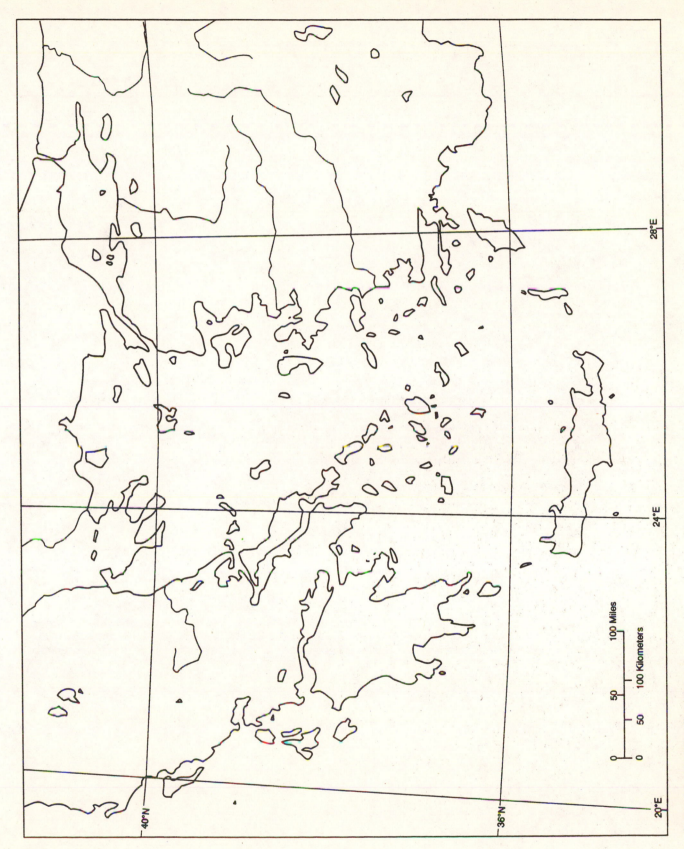

Exercise 10: The Early Aegean

40°N

36°N

20°E

24°E

28°E

100 Miles

100 Kilometers

0   50   100

0   50   100

XI. ANCIENT GREECE

In the eighth century B.C. the Greeks began to emerge from the Dark Age which followed the collapse of the Mycenaean Bronze Age civilization. The patterns, institutions and cultural achievements of these people would have an impact much greater than might have been expected, given their small numbers and limited resources. The Greek Peninsula south of Thessaly and Macedonia is a very small area measuring scarcely two hundred miles north to south and east to west.

Attica, in east central Greece, and Laconia, and Messenia in the southern Peloponnesus, are exceptions in a general pattern of poor soil and limited arable land. Only about twenty percent of the territory overall is suitable for agriculture. The mountainous nature of the terrain inhibited travel and communication as well. There are no major year-round river systems in Greece and seasonal rainfall provides the necessary moisture in a rather dry climate. Cereal grains were supplemented by olives, figs, small game, and fish. Only small communities could maintain any degree of self-sufficiency. Fifth-century Athens, with a population of three hundred thousand (including slaves and *metics*), came to be heavily dependent on imported grain. Sparta's deliberate political and economic policy of isolation and self-sufficiency was achieved only through the subjugation and enslavement of her neighbors in Laconia and Messenia.

Competition for land and internal political, economic, and social tensions forced many Greeks into overseas activities. The early lead taken by Corinth, Argos, Megara, and Chalcis was taken up by Greeks in Ionia, in western Asia Minor. Several generations contributed to the expansion and exploration which resulted in the opening of the northern Aegean, the Black Sea, North Africa, and the western Mediterranean. In the west, southern Italy, eastern Sicily, southern France, and even parts of Spain were major areas of Greek settlement. These early trading posts and migrant colonies relieved political pressures at home and had a profound impact abroad.

Competition with the equally aggressive Phoenicians could be quite vigorous, but opportunities justified the risks in the Etruscan market in Italy or among the indigenous peoples of Sicily and Gaul. Syracuse in Sicily and Miletus in Ionia came to rival the homeland Greek states in their power and influence. Corinth used its location to dominate the east-west trade through the Gulf. Byzantium on the Bosphorus was also in a perfect position at the entrance to the Black Sea to exploit the potential in that region. The tide-free Mediterranean and Aegean were easily navigable during the summer season and the numerous islands (some two thousand) further facilitated overseas commerce.

At home or abroad the achievement of the Greeks was tempered with political turmoil. Numerous variations on the political ideal of autonomy emerged. By 500 B.C. Sparta took its place as a militaristic agrarian-based community at the head of a defensive alliance called the Peloponnesian League. Athenian rivalry with Sparta in the aftermath of the Great War with Persia turned the anti-Persian Delian League into an empire under the ambitious Pericles.

A century that began with the realization of the world's first democracy and defeat of Persian tyranny culminated in the tragedy of the Peloponnesian War. The Greeks, whose unlimited vision took them to new frontiers in philosophy, science, and arts and letters, proved short-sighted when it came to any political scheme beyond the small-scale city-state. The rivalry, suspicion, envy, and pride that characterized the Athenian-Spartan conflict demonstrated the limitations of the polis idealized by Pericles.

EXERCISE 11
ANCIENT GREECE

I. **MAKING THE MAP**

    1.   Locate and label the Mediterranean Sea, the Aegean Sea, the Black Sea, the Ionian Sea, the Adriatic Sea, the Sea of Marmara.

    2.   Locate and label Asia Minor, Africa, Egypt, Phoenicia, Syria, Italy, the Iberian Peninsula.

    3.   Locate and label Laconia, Attica, Messenia, Argolis, Thessaly, Macedonia, Ionia, Thrace, Euboea. Color each a different color.

    4.   Locate and label Naxos, Delos, Samos, Chios, Corfu, Lesbos, Rhodes, Sicily, Salamis.

    5.   Locate with a black dot and label Athens, Corinth, Sparta, Argos, Delphi, Olympia, Thebes, Miletus, Halicarnassus, Byzantium, Sardis, Tyre, Piraeus.

    6.   Locate with a black dot and label Carthage, Syracuse, Massilia, Naukratis, Al Mina, Naples, Cyrene.

II. **READING THE MAP**

    1.   Entrance to the Black Sea from the Aegean is through the _____ and _____.

    2.   The three large islands off the west and south coast of Italy are _____, _____, and _____.

    3.   The most important Phoenician settlement in North Africa was _____.

    4.   The approximate distance between Sparta and Athens is _____.

III. **UNDERSTANDING THE MAP**

    1.   In addition to the indigenous population, who were the major competitors of the Greeks in Sicily?

    2.   What was the large empire the Greeks faced to their east in Asia Minor in the sixth and fifth centuries?

    3.   Name the general areas where Greeks made a significant impact in the era of colonization and expansion.

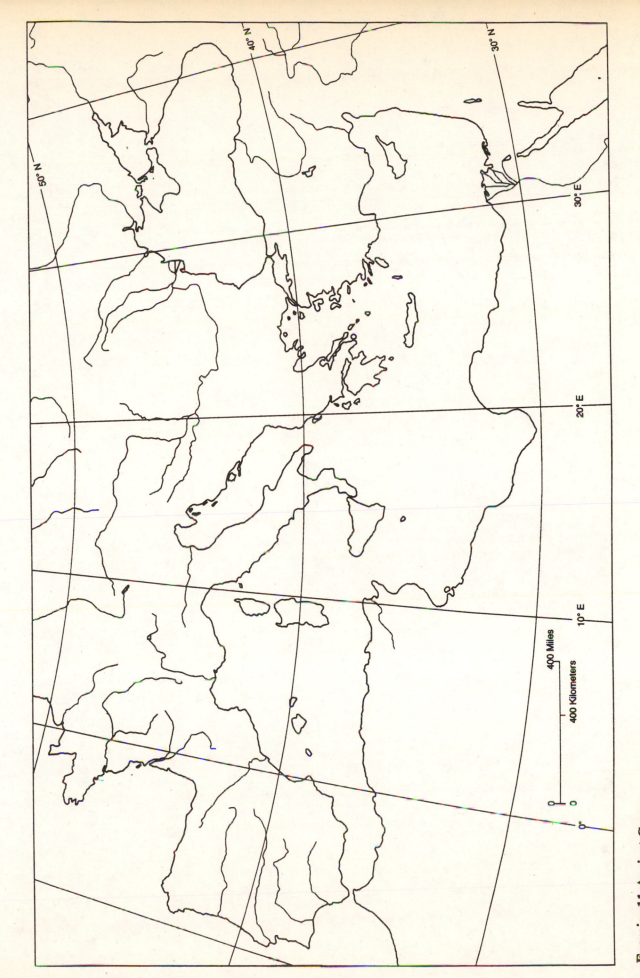

Exercise 11: Ancient Greece

400 Miles

400 Kilometers

0° · 10° E · 20° E · 30° E

30° N · 40° N · 50° N

47

XII. ALEXANDER THE GREAT AND THE HELLENISTIC AGE

In the fourth century, Macedonia, under Philip and his son, Alexander, created a powerful alternative to the narrow particularism of the autonomous Greek city-state. While the Athenians, Thebans, Spartans, and Persians intrigued and fought over territorial claims and allegiances, Philip put together a powerful army and unified kingdom with the capital at Pella. Traditionally dismissed by the Greeks as barbarians, the Macedonians moved successfully into Thessaly, Thrace, and into Greece. At the time of his assassination in 336 B.C. Philip had settled on a plan of world conquest. Alexander succeeded his father, put Macedonian and Greek affairs in order, and launched his campaign against Persia. His exploits took him and his mixed Greek-Macedonian army to Asia Minor, Phoenicia, Palestine, Egypt, Mesopotamia, and beyond the heartland to Persia, as far east as Afghanistan and India. All in all his conquests stretched from the Adriatic Sea in the west to the Indus River Valley in the east. His forces moved into the foothills of the Caucasus Mountains south to the shores of the Persian Gulf and the Arabian Sea. Battle after battle and adventure after adventure drove him over vast deserts, into rugged mountains, and across formidable rivers. Whether this great adventure was the work of a visionary or an egocentric conqueror continues to be debated. His conquests did usher in a new era.

The polis gave way to the cosmopolis in a new age of Greek civilization as Europe and Asia were joined. Political decisions were in the hands of Alexander's successors as they fought to determine if the future would be based on a unified new empire or separatist kingdoms. The Hellenistic world was no less turbulent or more peaceful than previous eras, but there was a tremendous growth in trade and wealth in a culturally unified world. Corinth, Rhodes, Miletus, and Ephesus flourished and grew. Athens, Pergamon, Alexandria in Egypt, Antioch in Syria, Ceos, Samos, and Syracuse were centers for development in the arts and sciences. A Greek core was planted in over seventy cities founded by these ambitious monarchs. The Greek language became the universal tongue and Greek merchants, officials, and mercenaries sought opportunity in this expanded world.

A kind of balance of power was worked out early in the third century with the Antigonids in Macedonia, the Seleucids in Asia Minor and the Ptolemys in Egypt. Of these, the Seleucid domains in Asia administered from Seleucia were the most extensive and Ptolemaic Egypt was the most cohesive. Both the Ptolemys and Seleucids utilized and refined the age-old systems they found in place in their respective kingdoms. Smaller Hellenized kingdoms such as Bithnyia, Pergamon and Pontus, among others, emerged in western and northern Asia Minor in the third and second centuries B.C. Mainland Greeks in the third century continued under a kind of Macedonian protectorate and produced a variety of confederations, alliances, and leagues and even a type of friend of federalism. Eventually two new powers, Rome in the West and the Parthians in the East, would become embroiled in the complicated dynastic quarrels, and political, military, and diplomatic struggles of the Hellenistic world. One-by-one over the second and first centuries B.C., Macedonia, the Seleucid Empire, the Greek mainland, the kingdoms of Asia Minor, and Ptolemaic Egypt fell into the Roman orbit.

EXERCISE 12
ALEXANDER THE GREAT AND THE HELLENISTIC AGE

I.   MAKING THE MAP

1.   Locate and label Macedonia, Persia, Asia Minor, Egypt, Bactria, Pontus, Pergamon, Syria, Mesopotamia, Babylonia.
2.   Locate and label the Mediterranean Sea, the Black Sea, the Caspian Sea, the Aral Sea, the Persian Gulf.
3.   Locate and label the Caucasus Mountains, the Zagros Mountains, the Hindu Kush.
4.   Locate and label the Nile River, the Tigris River, the Euphrates River, the Indus River, the Jaxartes River, the Oxus River.
5.   Locate with a black dot and label Athens, Pella, Thebes, Alexandria, Sardis, Babylon, Antioch, Persepolis, Susa, Ecbatana, Granicus, Issus, Tyre.
6.   With a thick black line, show the boundaries of the area covered by Alexander's empire at the time of his death.
7.   Color in red the area of the Antigonid Kingdom; color in blue the area of the Seleucid Kingdom; color in yellow the area of the Ptolemaic Kingdom, (300 B.C.).

II.   READING THE MAP

1.   The empire of Alexander was bordered on the south by the _____ Gulf and the _____ Sea.
2.   The Ptolemaic Kingdom was centered in the ancient kingdom of _____.
3.   Ptolemaic-Seleucid rivalry was concentrated mainly in _____ and _____.
4.   The two large bodies of water to the north of Alexander's empire are the _____ Sea and the _____ Sea.
5.   The capital city of the Ptolemaic Kingdom was _____.
6.   The capital of the Seleucid Kingdom was _____.

III.   UNDERSTANDING THE MAP

1.   Name several important states that emerged in Asia Minor to replace the Antigonid Kingdom.
2.   What city in Egypt became one of the most important cultural centers of the Hellenistic world?
3.   What empire developed to the east of the Seleucid territories beyond the Indus following Alexander's death?

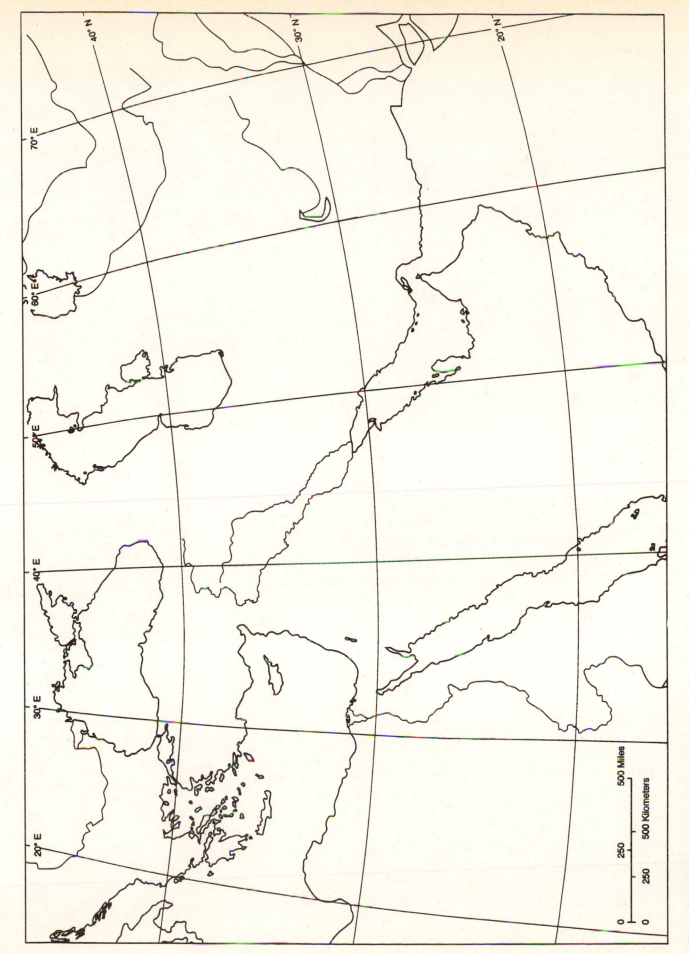

Exercise 12: Alexander the Great and the Hellenistic Age

XIII. CHINA'S STRUGGLE FOR CULTURAL AND POLITICAL UNITY,
400 B.C.–A.D. 400

In the fourth and third centuries B.C. the former vassal states of the Eastern Chou (Zhou) became independent rival states. There were seven major entities in all. The largest area was the Ch'u, which ran west to east across the Yangtze River. The Han and Wei in northcentral China were relatively small units. The Chao and Yen stretched across the northern frontiers. The state of Chi was located in the east on the Yellow Sea. Ch'in (Qin) lay far to the west on the frontier beyond the Yellow River. The Chi, Ch'u, Han, and Wei, as older organized centers, enjoyed some advantage in the fourth century. It was, however, the Ch'in on the northwest frontier that emerged to dominate all of China in the later part of the third century to bring the era of Warring States to a close. The Ch'in leader, who made himself emperor as Ch'in Shih Huang Ti, brought together a strong tradition of capable political and military leaders originating in the turbulent frontier region of the Ch'in. With a strong loyal army, he ruthlessly destroyed the feudal powers of the nobility and eliminated all opposition to promote order and stability. His reforms included a uniform system of weights and measures, money, and a common script for all his realm. The territory was divided into departments or commanderies headed by a civil and a military official delegated by the emperor. The administration instituted uniform legal and fiscal principals and practices as well. Feudal patterns of land tenure, slave labor, and military obligations were all abolished to strengthen the economy, agricultural production, and security of the empire. The imperial unity established by the Ch'in would remain an ideal in the Chinese tradition from this point forward. The Great Wall was a symbolic statement of the territorial integrity of the empire. The emperor improved and expanded this northern barrier on a grand scale in operations purported to have cost one million lives. Other even more practical public works projects included networks of roads, canals, and irrigation systems.

For all its successes the harsh authoritarian policies of the Ch'in proved too demanding and ultimately lacked consensus. Troubles arose after the emperor's death in 210 B.C. Order was to be restored from the chaos that followed by a new dynasty, the Han. The Han leaders built on the best of the Ch'in foundations. The administration of a land of some sixty million people required a strong and well-organized administration. Consensus and efficiency replaced brute force. Under Wu Ti (d. 87 B.C.) the Eastern or Former Han dynasty reached its peak. Tax collection, irrigation and canal projects, and overland transport were effectively implemented by the centralized bureaucracy. A canal some seventy miles in length connected the capital Ch'ang-An to the Yellow River. The capital had a fifteen mile perimeter protected by earthen walls with a dozen gates. Ch'ang-An was the seat of the imperial court and major markets. Imperial hunting preserves and lush parks were located outside the walls. The population has been estimated at 250,000 and included foreign traders from Greece, Persia, and India. Chinese silk and other goods were passed to the west on to Parthia and Rome. China was a major market for wool, glass, pearls, horses, and other goods in this prosperous period. An imperial monopoly controlled the vitally important production of iron for tools and weapons through state foundaries. Chinese expansion in the southeast developed the area around Canton on the Pearl River and beyond into Vietnam. To the north, incursions into southern Manchuria and northern Korea proved quite successful. The Han borders were stabilized at the northern frontiers where the Huns had been a continual problem.

Descendants of the original Han leaders breathed nearly two centuries of additional vitality into China's imperial traditions in the Later or Eastern Han. Loyang became the capital and the territorial boundaries of the empire were strengthened and restored. Much economic activity passed into private hands and overseas trade grew. The urban and merchant classes came to be wealthier and more powerful as central political and economic controls were relaxed. Court struggles, continued agrarian crises, frontier problems, and, finally, full scale rebellion in the Yellow Turban uprisings destroyed Han unity. The empire broke up into three regional states and China would not be unified again for nearly four centuries.

EXERCISE 13
CHINA'S STRUGGLE FOR CULTURAL AND POLITICAL UNITY,
400 B.C.–A.D. 400

I. MAKING THE MAP

1. Locate and label the Yangtze River, the Yellow River, the Yellow Sea, the East China Sea, the West River.
2. Locate and label Manchuria, Mongolia, Korea, Tibet.
3. Locate and show in red the approximate area of the Ch'u and in blue the Ch'in (Qin).
4. Draw the approximate boundary lines of the Han Empire.
5. Locate and label the states of Han, Zhao, Wei, Yan, Chi (Qi), and Chu.
6. Locate with a black dot and label Ch'ang-An, Loyang, Yen, Pa, Wu.
7. Show the approximate line of the Great Wall *ca.* A.D. 200.

II. READING THE MAP

1. China's initial move toward unity had its origins in Chang and Zhou eras located in the basin of the _____ River in _____ China.
2. The epoch of the Warring States was brought to a close by the growth of the _____.
3. The six states absorbed and unified by the Ch'in (Qin) were the _____, _____, _____, _____, _____, and _____.
4. Among these states the largest was the _____.
5. The Han Empire (206 B.C.–A.D. 250) extended from the _____ Ocean westward as far as the _____ Mountain Range.
6. Among the important regions incorporated by the Han, _____ was located to the northeast.
7. The distance from Tun-huang along the Great Wall to the Pacific is approximately _____ miles.

III. UNDERSTANDING THE MAP

1. Name some of the important foreign contacts made by China during the Han era.
2. What was the purpose of the Great Wall and when did it take its basic form?
3. Describe the main administrative problems faced by China during the Zhou (Chou) and the Ch'in.
4. The Han Empire was eventually troubled by serious threats. What form did they take and from what region did the external problems originate?

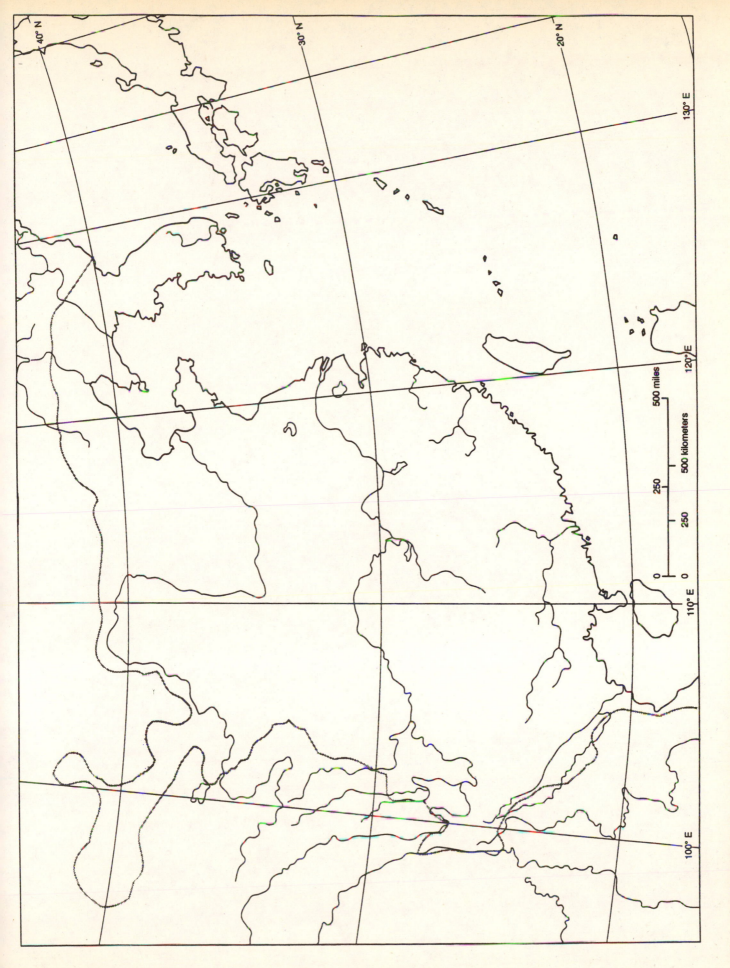

Exercise 13: China's Struggle for Cultural and Political Unity

By about 1000 B.C. significant advances were being made in the area of the Yamuna River and Upper Ganges River. At Hastinapur and Ahicctra to the southeast, small towns were emerging. Aryan-speaking migrants had mixed with Harappan and other Indian groups to dominate northern India down to the Vindhya Range in the area of the Narbada Valley. In what is called the Late Vedic period, the use of iron tools aided greatly in land clearing and agriculture. In the area known as Hindustan, from modern Delhi east to the north of the Ganges at the Bay of Bengal, the cultivation of rice was a major factor in population growth and the formation of cities. By 600 B.C. as many as sixteen separate well-organized states competed among themselves for survival and growth. The cities were defended by mud brick walls. Kausamdhi on the middle Ganges, and Ujjain, some distance to the southwest, are two of many found in the region.

Over the course of the fifth century continued struggles resulted in the consolidation of the many states into four, until finally all were united into what would be the core of India's first empire controlled by the kingdom of Magadha. Nepal to the north and much of the Deccan to the south would eventually be incorporated into this empire under Ashoka in the third century B.C. The Nanda dynasty had established its capital at Pataliputra, which could control the Ganges trade routes. In the Mauryan period it became a large and rich administrative center defended by strong walls. It is said to have extended some eight or more miles along the shores of the Ganges.

In the fourth century dramatic changes occurred in the Indus River area as well. Alexander the Great penetrated the area in his conquest. Alexander defeated King Porus on the Hydaspes and subjugated Ghandara. The neighboring area to the west, Bactria, came to be an important source of Greek cultural influence on India. Tradition suggests that it was after a meeting with Alexander that Chandragupta was inspired to take the Magadha throne in 321 and create his own empire. He moved northwest as far as the Indus River once Alexander had left, and then moved south occupying large parts of central India to the Narbada River. He returned to the northwest to defeat Seleucus Nicator and annex major territories west of the Hindu Kush range in the region of Afghanistan. Chandragupta's son and grandson, Asoka, enlarged the empire even more to include much of the subcontinent. The area of Kalinga on the Bay of Bengal was a major acquisition.

The territories controlled by Ashoka were efficiently managed and the source of great income. Trade added to the wealth at the government's disposal. The agricultural base of the economy was supplemented by trade from Tamluk, at the Ganges mouth, upriver and along overland routes to Taxila and Charsadda farther north. Eventually a substantial maritime trade developed to the south utilizing the monsoon winds. There is clear evidence, for instance, of Roman trade at Kaverippattinam and Arikamedur on India's southeastern shores.

Another testament to Ashoka's power is to be found in the large number of epigraphic edicts or pronouncements he had placed throughout his realm. These moral and ethical codes based on Buddhist principles were carved on monuments and rock faces and designed to provide a common base for the various cultural and ethnic elements in this territory. After Ashoka's death, decline set in and India was subjected to invasions such as those of the Greeks from Bactria and then the Yüeh-Chih, whose unification produced the Kushan Empire in northwest India in the first century A.D. In the south states such as Chola, Pandya, and Pallava, on the mainland, and Sinhalas and Tamils, on Ceylon, some twenty miles across the Palk Strait, were distinctive and important kingdoms as well.

EXERCISE 14
INDIA, *CA.* 700–200 B.C.: KINGDOMS AND EMPIRE

I.   MAKING THE MAP

1.   Locate and label the Arabian Sea, the Bay of Bengal, the Indian Ocean.
2.   Locate and label the Indus River, the Ganges River, the Bramaputra River.
3.   Locate and label the Himalaya Mountains, the Hindu Kush, the Vindhya Mountains, the Tibetan Plateau, the Thar Desert, the Sulaiman Range.
4.   Locate and label the areas of Kashmir, Punjab, Ghandara, Magadha, Kalinga, Sind, Tamil Land, Ceylon.
5.   Locate with a black dot and label Pataliputra.
6.   Shade in the area of Ashoka's empire.

II.   READING THE MAP

1.   What is the approximate distance in miles from Kashmir to the southern tip of India?
2.   The Ganges River originates in the foothills of the _____ Mountains and flows into the _____.
3.   The Indus River flows generally _____ to _____ and into the _____ Sea.

III.   UNDERSTANDING THE MAP

1.   What geographical features of India tended to inhibit political unity?
2.   Name the two modern states located on the eastern and western borders of India.
3.   What types of agricultural products were typical of the various regions of India?
4.   What was the impact of invaders from outside India in the fourth century B.C.?
5.   Where was the administrative and cultural center of Mauryan India in the third century B.C.?

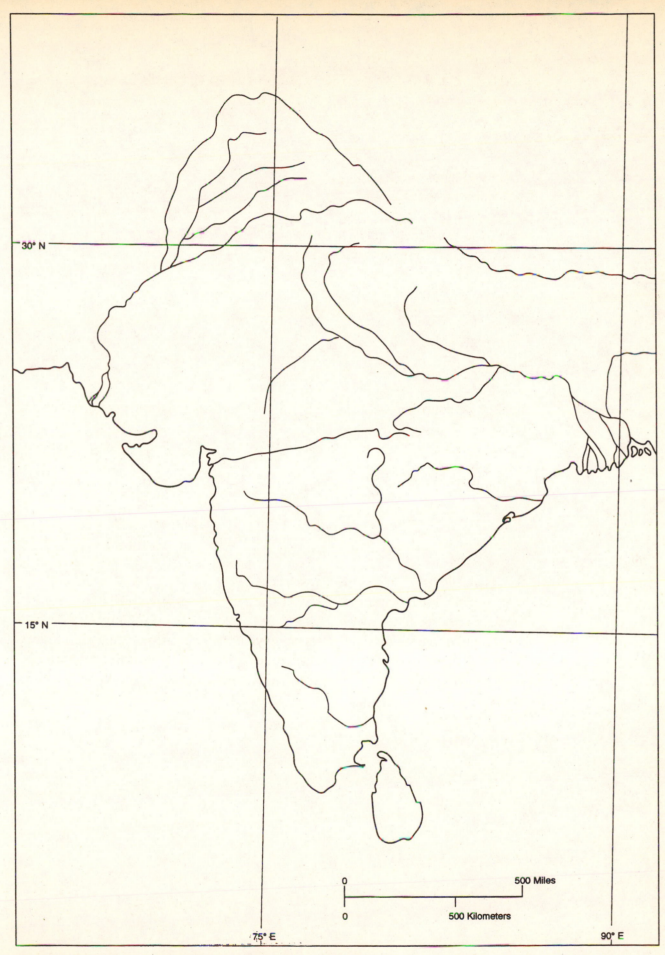

Exercise 14: India, ca 700-300 B.C.: Kingdoms and Empire

XV. ROME, ITALY AND EMPIRE

The Italian Peninsula measures about seven hundred and fifty miles from north to south. It varies from one hundred to one hundred and fifty miles in width. The dominant feature of this European extension into the Mediterranean Sea is the Apennine Mountain Range. The mountains are a continuous extension of the Alps and form a kind of backbone of the peninsula. The mountains here do not compartmentalize Italy as they do in Greece and the passage of peoples here is not so difficult. To the south of the peninsula lies the largest island of the Mediterranean, Sicily, which is just one hundred miles distant from Africa. To the east is the Adriatic Sea whose shore has few harbors. To the west is the Tyrrhenian Sea with two large islands, Corsica and Sardinia. The southwest region of Italy has a number of good harbors including Cumae and Naples. Rome itself is located some eighteen miles up the Tiber from the coast. In the north, the Po and Arno rivers water large agricultural areas. In southcentral Italy Latium and Campania have good soil. The central Mediterranean region is particularly prone to heavy earthquakes. Mount Aetna in Sicily and Mount Vesuvius on the mainland are active volcanoes. Italy's general geographical and cultural orientation was westward and in part explains its relatively late development.

By 1500 B.C. Indo-European speaking invaders entered the Italian Peninsula blending with or displacing previous inhabitants. It was the bronze age Apennine culture which introduced advanced copper and bronze technology to the area. Iron working technology and other advances came with the Villanovan culture about 1000 B.C. The Latins settled in west central Italy. Other immigrants, the Etruscans (possibly from Asia Minor), settled in Etruria to the northwest. From the eighth century B.C. to the early fifth they built an empire from the Po Valley south to Campania and from the Tyrrhenian Sea east to the shores of the Adriatic. Concurrently the Greeks settled in autonomous city-states south of Rome and were major contributors to Roman and Etruscan political, cultural and economic development. Rome itself was initially only one small community among many in Latium. Carthage, in North Africa, and numerous other Phoenician settlements in western Sicily formed a major power in the western Mediterranean.

Rome's centuries-long struggle for survival led her on a path that culminated in a Republic for Romans and a Confederation with her allies in Italy. In the process, Rome took on her powerful neighbors to the west and east to create an empire abroad. The growing pains of becoming a world power and the crisis of civil war in Italy were resolved with the creation of the Augustan Principate. Roman control extended from the British Isles, Spain, and Gaul on the Atlantic, to Macedonia, Greece, Asia Minor, and Mesopotamia, as far as the Euphrates River in the east. The Rhine and Danube rivers formed the empire's continental boundaries (except for Dacia). The North African provinces from Egypt to the Strait of Gibraltar made up the southern limits of the Empire. Rome, with a population of perhaps one million was the capital of an Empire of one hundred million in the first and second centuries A.D. Great cities of the east such as Alexandria, Ephesus, and Antioch flourished in this era. To the west, development of new centers such as Lyon, Treves, and Cologne, serving military and commercial functions, became key to the Romanization process. The agricultural base of the economy was enriched by commerce, government requirements, and a money economy. A widespread system of roads, riverways, and harbors facilitated the exchange of goods until the combined burdens of barbarian enemies, economic crises, and leadership weaknesses surfaced in the third century. It was after the crises of the third century that a new era was inaugurated with the creation of a second capital of an administratively divided empire located at Byzantium (Constantinople).

EXERCISE 15
ROME, ITALY AND EMPIRE

I.   **MAKING THE MAP**

1.   Locate and label the Mediterranean Sea, the Black Sea, the Tyrrhenian Sea, the Adriatic Sea, the Red Sea, the Caspian Sea, the English Channel, the Strait of Gibraltar, the Atlantic Ocean.
2.   Locate and label the Tiber River, the Po River, the Rhine River, the Danube River, the Nile River, the Tigris River, the Euphrates River.
3.   Locate and label the Apennine Mountains, the Alps, the Pyrenees Mountains.
4.   Locate and label Italy, Spain, Gaul, Britain, Achaea, Macedonia, Dacia, Egypt, Libya, Numidia, Judaea, Thrace, Dalmatia.
5.   Locate and label Latium, Etruria, Campania, Magna Graecia (Greater Greece), Sicily, Sardinia, Corsica.
6.   Locate with a black dot and label Rome, Ostia, Syracuse, Carthage, Veii, Messina, Corinth, Athens, Alexandria, Byzantium, Antioch, Massilia.

II.   **READING THE MAP**

1.   The massive mountain range to the immediate north of the Italian Peninsula is called the _____.
2.   The city of Rome is located in _____ Italy on the _____ River.
3.   Early Italy was dominated by the powerful and well-organized _____ to the north of Rome and the _____ to the south.
4.   The mountain chain running down the center of Italy is the _____ Range.
5.   The large island off the south coast of Italy is _____.
6.   The approximate distance in miles from Rome to Carthage is _____.

III.   **UNDERSTANDING THE MAP**

1.   List the strategic advantages inherent in Rome's location in Italy and Italy's position in the Mediterranean.
2.   What was the major threat Rome faced in the western Mediterranean in the third and second centuries B.C. and where was it located?
3.   What rivers formed the natural boundaries of the Roman Empire in continental Europe?
4.   What territory did Rome claim off the northwest coast of Europe?
5.   Name the Roman province located north of the Danube River in Eastern Europe. What is the name of the modern state in this region?
6.   What were the major groups limiting Roman expansion in North Africa, continental Europe, and the area of the Tigris and Euphrates rivers?

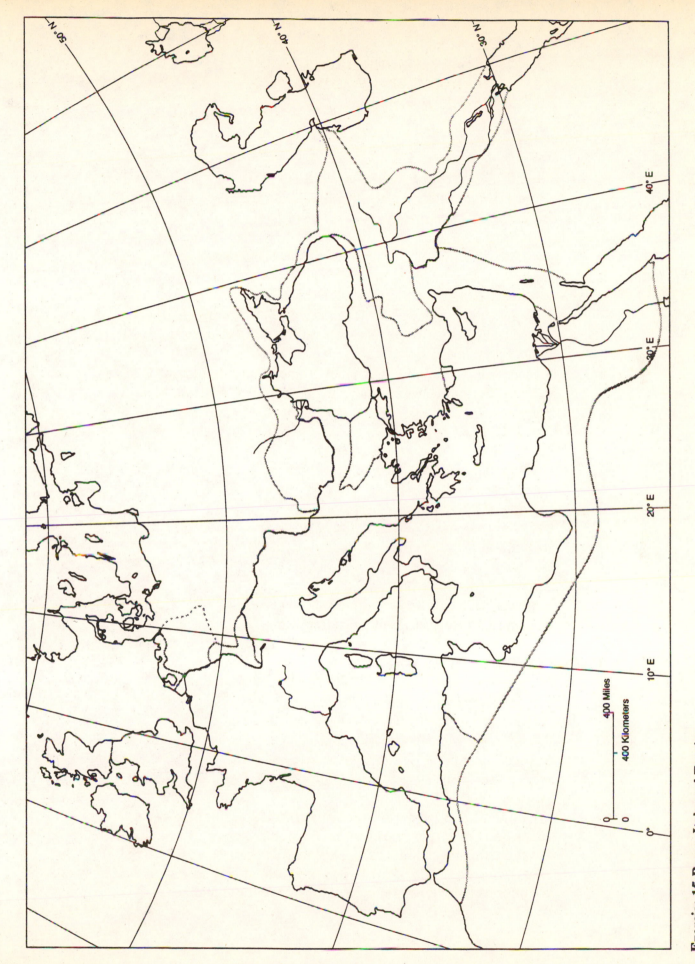

Exercise 15: Rome, Italy and Empire

400 Miles

400 Kilometers

0

0

0° 10° E 20° E 30° E 40° E

30° N 40° N 50° N

65

XVI. ROME, BYZANTIUM AND THE BARBARIANS

As early as the third century A.D., changes in climate and population growth, along with aggression by pastoral nomads, set in motion developments that would transform Europe and Asia. In subsequent centuries, from China, across central Asia, to India, Persia, and the Roman Empire, the ethnic and political maps would be redrawn. A troubled West Roman Empire was dismantled by wave after wave of Germanic invaders on the move from their homelands to the north and east. Theodoric established an Ostrogothic kingdom in Italy and the regions at the head of the Adriatic in the late fifth century. Visigoths founded a kingdom in Spain. The Vandals, under Gaiseric in the 440s, carved out a kingdom in North Africa and launched maritime attacks against Rome. The British Isles were overrun by Angles and Saxons from the continent. In the fourth and fifth centuries central Asian Huns ranged deep into Gaul before their efforts collapsed following the death of their leader Attila. Burgundians and Franks would replace them in Gaul. In the seventh and eighth centuries the Merovingian and Carolingian Franks put together a powerful coalition with the blessing of the Church in the form of the Holy Roman Empire. This Germanic creation included Gaul, much of central Germany, and half of Italy. At its peak, the time of Charlemagne's death in 814, it was a substantial challenger to the East Roman Empire.

The strengths of the East Roman Empire and its capital were tested and proved sound. Constantinople was located on the site of the old Greek city of Byzantium (hence the later name for the East Roman Empire: Byzantine). On the Bosphorus connecting the Aegean and Black Sea, it was ideally located for defense, commerce and administration. The Emperor Justinian (d. 565) even succeeded in temporarily reuniting the empire. He defeated the Goths in Italy, the Vandals in Africa, and held off a rejuvenated Persian Empire to the east. His victorious generals even recovered a bit of Spain from the Visigoths. Justinian's accomplishments weakened the empire, rather than restoring it, in the long run, however. New invaders waited in the wings for their chance at conquest. Lombards moved into Italy and the Franks into Gaul. In the seventh and eighth centuries the Arabs began a movement which would defeat the Persians, overwhelm Roman territories in Syria, Palestine, Egypt, North Africa and subdue most of Spain. Constantinople, however, held out not only against Arabs but Bulgars and Slavs as well, who launched attack after attack in the seventh and eighth centuries. The central Asian Bulgars and Slavic groups (pushed by Avars) were successful in establishing kingdoms in Eastern Europe which had been part of the Roman Empire. Among other developments in the West a Germanic/Christian/Roman synthesis would perpetuate, at least, the ideal of a Roman Empire. In the east, the East Roman or Byzantine Empire remained vital for one thousand years until the Turkish conquest.

In the West the economy of the Roman Empire was reduced to largely subsistence-level agricultural patterns. A decentralized barter-based system evolved as urban centers and transportation and communication networks failed. Agriculture was the basis for the economy in the East, of course, but a money economy and widespread overseas commerce persisted. Guilds of craftsmen and artisans produced goods marketed in the capital and provincial cities. Luxury goods such as silk came from the Far East until it was produced in Constantinople itself. The capital was the focal point of East-West trade from Asia to the Middle East and to Europe. Grain, wine, olive oil, and dairy products were relatively abundant. A civil autocracy and eventually a land-based military aristocracy were two major components that evolved to meet the empire's administrative and defense needs.

EXERCISE 16
ROME, BYZANTIUM AND BARBARIANS

I.   MAKING THE MAP

1.   Locate and label the Atlantic Ocean, the North Sea, the Baltic Sea, the Black Sea, the Mediterranean Sea, the Caspian Sea, the English Channel, the Strait of Gibraltar, the Bosphorus.
2.   Locate and label the Rhine River, the Danube River, the Dnieper River.
3.   Locate and label the Alps Mountains, the Pyrenees Mountains, the Carpathian Mountains.
4.   Locate with a black dot and label Rome, Constantinople, Milan, Trier, Jerusalem, Antioch, Carthage, Nicaea, Damascus, Cordova, Hippo, Seville, Ravenna, Tours.
5.   Show in yellow the territory of the East Roman (Byzantine) Empire *ca.* A.D. 500.
6.   Locate and label the Vandal Kingdom under Gaiseric.
7.   Locate and label the Ostrogothic Kingdom under Theodoric.

II.   READING THE MAP

1.   In the fourth and fifth centuries A.D. the Roman province of Britain was ceded to the _____ and _____ from continental Europe.
2.   The Visigothic Kingdom was established in the area of the _____ Peninsula.
3.   The capital of the Vandal Kingdom was established at _____ in the area originally known as _____.
4.   The capital of the East Roman Empire was called _____ and located on the European side of the _____.
5.   The major threat to the East Roman Empire under Justinian from the east was the _____ Empire.
6.   The original homeland of the Germanic peoples who invaded the Roman Empire was _____.

III.   UNDERSTANDING THE MAP

1.   What group of Germanic barbarians established itself as the major power in the former Roman province of Gaul?
2.   In what ways did the Huns differ from the other barbarian invaders of Europe?
3.   What were some of the advantages of Constantinople as a site of government in the East Roman Empire?
4.   Name several cities that emerged as important cultural and intellectual centers in the east as the barbarians overran the western half of the Empire.

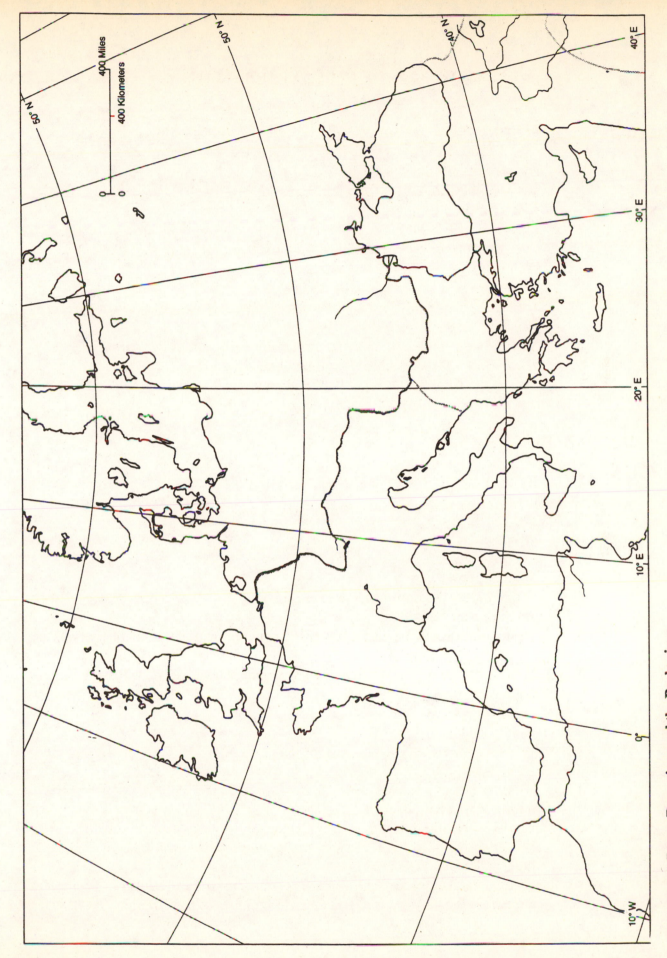

Exercise 16: Rome, Byzantium and the Barbarians

XVII. ARAB EXPANSION AND THE ISLAMIC WORLD, A.D. 570 - 800

Islam had its origins in the city of Mecca on the western coast of the Arabian Peninsula. Here, and in the city of Medina (Yathrib), about 250 miles due north, Mohammed and his followers among the Koraysh founded this new monotheistic faith. Drawing on Arab, Jewish, and Christian traditions, Mohammed and Islam energized the Semetic-speaking Arabs into a phenomenal expansionist movement with far-reaching consequences.

The Arabian Peninsula is overall an inhospitable area. This largely desert region, about one-third the size of the United States is bordered by the Red Sea on the west, the Gulf of Aden, the Arabian Sea, and the Persian Gulf on the south and east. A range of mountains with peaks up to nine thousand feet, the Hejag, runs just inland along the shore of the Red Sea from the Sinai Peninsula south to Yemen. A huge sand desert, the Rub al Khali, is located in the southern part of the region. The climate of the area is very dry with less than four inches of rainfall per year. Less than two percent of Arabia is arable.

In the sixth century, there were small kingdoms in the north and south. Those in the north had contacts with the Byzantine and Persian empires. Saba in the south is associated with the legendary Sheba. The majority of the interior population was nomadic following traditional tribal organization. They and their herds were dependent on the water found in the scattered oases. Mecca had a source of water and was a traditional religious center. It also owed its importance to its location relative to the main east-west routes from Central Asia and Persia to Africa. It was similarly favored on the northwest-southeast routes from the Mediterranean to India. Across the Red Sea, commercial contacts in Abyssinia were well established.

The religion of Islam took form through Mohammed, who saw himself as the last in a long line of prophets in the tradition of Judaism and Christianity. Islam proved to be a uniting factor among the Arabs so that within a few generations after Mohammed's death in 632, their horizons had moved far beyond the tribe and a kingdom to that of empire.

Initially, Arabia was united and administered from Medina. From this starting point, the religious goal, which was combined with military and political ambitions was projected beyond Arabia. The Byzantine and Persian states were tempting and vulnerable targets for expansion in the seventh century. These two empires had recently exhausted each other in a stand-off struggle of their own. Syria, Palestine, and Egypt had long-standing economic and religious quarrels with the Imperial Administration in Constantinople as well.

Success followed success as Arab armies moved into Syria and Palestine to the north and Mesopotamia and Persia to the east. Jerusalem, Damascus, Ctesiphon, Mosul, and Nehavend fell one after the other. The forces of Islam moved as far north as the Caucasus between the Caspian and Black seas by the mid seventh century. Despite internal dynastic and power struggles among Mohammed's successors, expansion continued.

By 640 Egypt had fallen, thus opening the Mediterranean Sea and North Africa to Arab advances. By the end of the century combined land and sea attacks were launched against Constantinople. Under the Omayads (661–750) the whole northern rim of Africa to the Maghreb was incorporated into the empire. From the Strait of Gibraltar Arab forces entered the Iberian Peninsula, defeated the

Visigoths, and crossed the Pyrenees into Gaul. They were, however, turned back by the Franks at Poitiers and Tours. Cordoba in Spain would emerge as an independent emirate after 750.

In the East, Arab-Islamic forces proved unstoppable until they reached the Hindu Kush and the Sind in northwest India. Expeditions launched from Mishapur in eastern Persia led to Merv, Bukhara, Samarkand, Kabul, and Multan on the Indus River. The Abbasid dynasty, founded in 750, moved the capital of this now vast territory from Damascus to Baghdad and ended the Arab monopoly in the Islamic Empire. Subsequently internal differences and leadership failures created a situation where numerous regional components emerged. In the populous cities, across the Mediterranean, Arabian Sea, Indian Ocean, and on the caravan routes through central Asia, the Islamic world was one of cultural and religious unity with strong economic ties. Direct or indirect commerce was eventually established from Africa through the Middle East to India, China, and Southwest Asia.

EXERCISE 17
ARAB EXPANSION AND THE ISLAMIC WORLD, A.D. 570– 800

I. MAKING THE MAP

1. Locate and label the Mediterranean Sea, the Atlantic Ocean, the Black Sea, the Arabian Sea, the Caspian Sea, the Aral Sea, the Red Sea, the Persian Gulf.
2. Locate and label the Indus River, the Danube River, the Tigris River, the Euphrates River, the Nile River, the Loire River.
3. Locate and label the Zagros Mountains, the Atlas Mountains, the Pyrenees Mountains, the Caucasus Mountains, the Sahara Desert.
4. Locate and label the Arabian Peninsula, Egypt, Persia (Iran), Anatolia, Afghanistan, Baluchistan, Iraq, Syria, Spain.
5. Locate and label Crete, Sicily, Cyprus, the Strait of Gibraltar, the Bosphorus.
6. Locate with a black dot and label Mecca, Medina, Constantinople, Tours, Cairo, Jerusalem, Baghdad, Damascus, Tripoli, Tangier, Tunis, Kabul, Merv, Samarkand.
7. Show in red the approximate area of the Byzantine Empire and in yellow the area of the Frankish Kingdom *ca.* A.D. 800.
8. Show by a heavy dark line the boundaries of the Islamic World as of A.D. 750.

II. READING THE MAP

1. What is the predominant natural feature of the Arabian Peninsula?
2. The major territorial acquisition of Islam in Europe was the territory of _____.
3. The first capital of the Arab-Islamic Empire was at _____ in _____.
4. By about A.D. 750 the Islamic Empire had expanded eastward to the _____ River.
5. The major non-European territorial component of the Byzantine Empire which survived the advance of Islam was _____.

III. UNDERSTANDING THE MAP

1. What natural formation served as a barrier between Islamic expansion in Spain and the Frankish Kingdom?
2. What advantages came to Islamic expansion with the conquest of Alexandria?
3. What large territorial empire confronted Arab expansion east of the Arabian Peninsula?
4. What cultural and economic elements combined to make Mecca important in the birth of Islam?

73

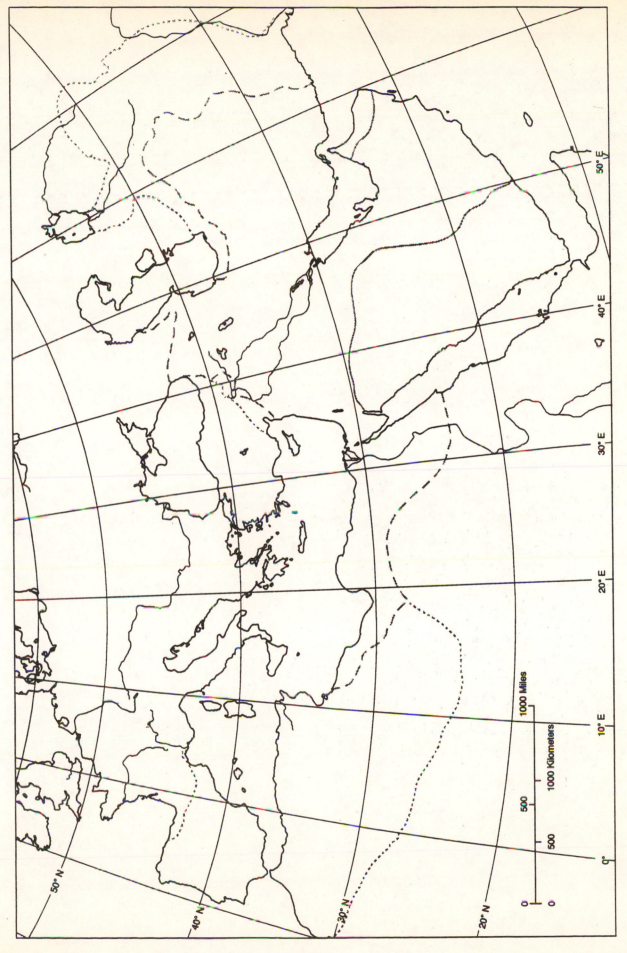

Exercise 17: Arab Expansion and the Islamic World, 570-800 A.D.

XVIII. ISLAM AND AFRICA: EAST AND WEST, A.D. 1000–1500

From the tenth through the fifteenth centuries, Africa saw the development of a variety of states and economic patterns. In the north, from the Red Sea to the Atlantic along the shores of the Mediterranean, the Fatimids, Ayynbids, and Mamelukes dominated Egypt. To the west, the Almohad and Almoravid empires emerged in the period from the eleventh through the thirteenth centuries. These Berber empires in the Maghreb followed the appearance of Islam in the region some three centuries before. In the area of the Horn of Africa west of the Red Sea across from the Arabian Peninsula, the Islamic state of Adal competed with the newly revived Christian Kingdom of Ethiopia.

Elsewhere on the continent new patterns emerged which reflected the stimulus to traditional centers of development. Major changes occurred in at least three regions. The centuries-old agricultural communities which had flourished in the African environment came to be greatly transformed through contacts with Islam and involvement with elements from the Mediterranean Sea, the Persian Gulf, and the Indian Ocean.

Ghana, located in the western area of the sub-Saharan Sudanic strip that runs from the Nile to the Atlantic, was one of the early states to emerge. Here in the area of the Senegal and Niger rivers, Kumbi Saleh, which was well located on the trade routes between the desert and the forest regions to the south, became a thriving city. Merchant-traveller camel caravans brought in luxury goods and salt in exchange for gold, hides, slaves, and cotton. Sigilmasa, across the Atlas Mountains to the north, was the Berber link in this flourishing trans-Saharan economy. It was Almoravid Berbers, in fact, who ended the great days of Ghana in the eleventh century. Mali, in the thirteenth century succeeded Ghana in the region.

Cities such as Gao, Jenné, and Timbuktu were important centers for a prosperous internal trade. Mali controlled the agriculturally productive Niger River and the gold-rich white Volta and Akan areas in the south. Eventually Mali's rule extended beyond the Senegal River to the shores of the Atlantic Ocean. Conversion to Islam widened the cultural and religious patterns of Mali to the broader Islamic world. By the end of the eleventh century, however, localism prevailed and the economic and political base of the Mali state eroded severely. The important city of Timbuktu fell to Tuareg Berbers from the north and Songhai seceded to form its own independent state. Songhai was centered on Gao and Timbuktu.

To the east city-states such as Zarina, Kano, and Katsina in the Hausa region developed as prosperous alternatives to a unified state or empire on the Ghana or Mali models. In the region of Lake Chad, farther to the north and east, Kanuri and Kanem-Bornu came to be significant centers of political and economic strength in the fourteenth and fifteenth centuries. The east coast of Africa was another important area where the Arab-Islamic catalyst resulted in major change. Agricultural communities from Mogadishu in the north to Mozambique in the south felt the impact of merchant travellers from Arabia and the Persian Gulf in the ninth and tenth centuries.

In the twelfth and thirteenth centuries Egyptian enterprise in the Red Sea opened a new, wider phase in commercial operations. India, Malaya, and Indonesia across the Indian Ocean came into the picture subsequently. Among east coast Swahili communities, the city-state, such as Mogadishu, Mombasa, Zanzibar, and Kilwa, became the typical political and economic unit. These port cities flourished as intermediaries between the interior of Africa, the Mediterranean, and Asia. Slaves and ivory were traded for iron products, cloth, and food. Here, as elsewhere, the acceptance of Islam cemented economic and cultural ties.

Zimbabwe, with its port city of Sofala, came to be an important state between 1100 and 1500. It had the population, the political organization, and the agricultural base on the highland plateau, just inland, to capitalize on coastal economic activities. Great Zimbabwe, with a population of over eighteen thousand, was the capital of a strong and rich state. There is ample evidence of wide long-distance trade to India, China, and Persia. Copper, gold, and ivory were vital exports from the region. The delicate ecology of the region contributed to the eventual decline of Zimbabwe in the fifteenth century. Overpopulation, mismanagement of the shallow soil, agriculture, and overgrazing appear to have taken their toll and left the system unable to deal with drought, famine, or epidemic disease.

EXERCISE 18
ISLAM AND AFRICA: EAST AND WEST, A.D. 1000–1500

I.   MAKING THE MAP

1. Locate and label the Mediterranean Sea, the Gulf of Guinea, the Red Sea, the Gulf of Aden.
2. Locate and label the Niger River, the Zambezi River, the Nile River, the Benue River, the Senegal River, the Gambia River, the Congo River, Lake Victoria, Lake Tanganyika.
3. Locate and label Madagascar, the Comoro Islands, the Sahara Desert, Egypt, Ethiopia, Arabia.
4. Locate with a black dot and label Mecca, Medina, Marrakech, Tangier, Kumbí Saleh, Sigilmasa, Gao, Jenné, Timbuktu.
5. Show in yellow the approximate area of Ghana at its greatest extent in the eleventh century.
6. Show by a dark line the approximate area covered by the state of Mali *ca.* 1240–1500.
7. Show the approximate border of Great Zimbabwe.
8. Locate with a black dot and label Mogadishu, Mombasa, Sofala, Zanzibar, Kilwa.

II.   READING THE MAP

1. The states of Ghana and Mali were located in the region of the upper _____ and _____ rivers.
2. Initial cultural and economic contacts between Arabs in North Africa and the Sahel area were by way of caravan routes south over the _____.
3. The town that developed as a base for the state of Ghana was _____.
4. Along with Gao and Jenné on the Upper _____ River, the city of _____ became a major center of the Mali world.
5. Merchants from Arabia and the Persian Gulf sailed across the _____ Ocean to exploit economic opportunities in East Africa.
6. Other areas of Arab economic and cultural expansion to the west were in _____, _____, and _____.
7. The Swahili towns along the east coast of Africa merged with _____, located to the interior south of the _____ River to form a major state in the thirteenth century.

III.   UNDERSTANDING THE MAP

1. What significant new element introduced by traders in North Africa facilitated trans-Saharan commerce?

2. What was the vital commodity that rivaled and even surpassed gold in its importance in the trans-Saharan trade?

3. Which city of southern Morocco was the main focus for the Ghana gold trade?

4. What was the basis for the prosperity of the Ghana state?

5. What West African state replaced Mali in the fourteenth and fifteenth centuries?

6. What was the characteristic form of the Swahili states on the east African coast and what was their role with respect to the interior?

7. What were the sources of economic prosperity for the state of Zimbabwe until the fifteenth century?

8. Roughly speaking, what regions of the African continent were most influenced by Islam?

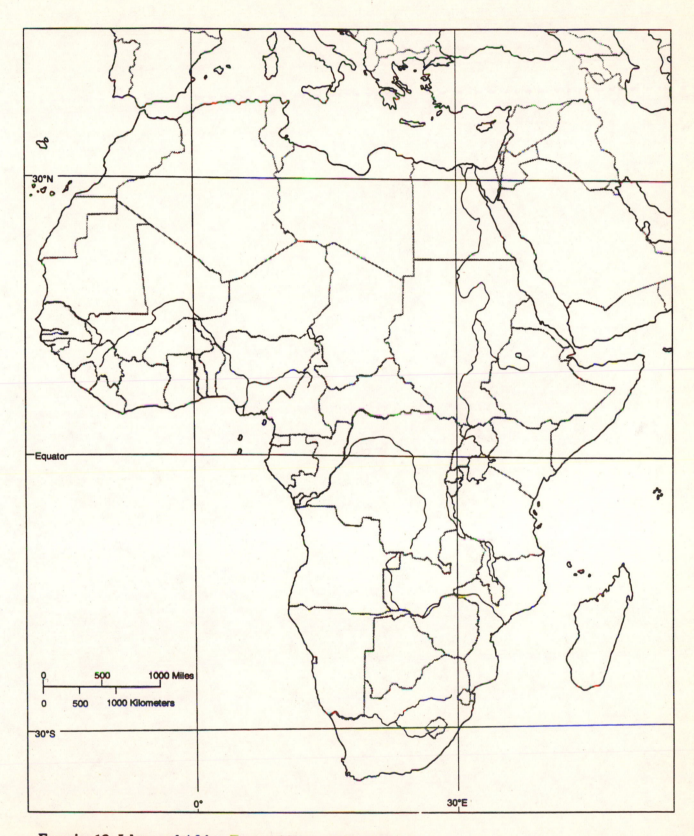

Exercise 18: Islam and Africa, East and West, 1000-1550 A.D.

XIX. T'ANG CHINA: UNITY AND EXPANSION, A.D. 618–907

The Sui dynasty unified China and brought an end to the era known as the Six Dynasties or Period of Disunion in 589. The Period of Disunion followed the collapse of the Han in 220 and China's invasion by a variety of northern barbarians. A new period of unity, prosperity, and expansion was opened with the Sui and extended by the T'ang from the seventh through the ninth centuries. The dormant ideal of unity for China was energetically revived and implemented with a variety of methods. The problem of regionalism was met with themes drawn from Taoism, Confucian teaching, and a broader version of Buddhism. A single common script for the many dialects of Chinese was another cultural and administrative unifying element. The Imperial or Grand Canal, some 1,400 miles in length, connected the Yellow River and the Yangtze at Hangchou (Hangzhou) and tied Peking (Beijing) of the north to the capital at Ch'ang-An. This 130-foot-wide water transport system with strategically located granaries, facilitated the movement and storage of grain for distribution and tax collection. It was paralleled by a Royal Road which served as land transport and communication. The reconstruction of the Great Wall was another practical public works project.

The Sui, however, expended considerable energy in futile attempts to annex territories to the northeast in the area of the Korean Peninsula. A combination of overly costly and ambitious military schemes and natural disasters brought the Sui to a troubled close and the T'ang picked up the pieces in 618. Under the T'ang, China would reach its greatest territorial limit. T'ang China was a highly centralized, well-administered state. The territory was administered by a well-organized bureaucracy in separate specialized governmental structures. This pattern, along with the merit system of exams for government service, became a standard feature of Chinese government for centuries to come. Provinces were subdivided into prefectures, sub-prefectures, and districts. All were staffed by government appointed officials from the capital in Ch'ang-An. At its peak, the great capital city had a combined population of over two million within and outside its defense walls.

A stable and productive peasantry was the basis for T'ang prosperity. In this period, rice culture was expanded to become a staple crop. Advanced agricultural technology permitted substantial development in the Yangtze River Valley to the south. T'ang ambitions also gave rise to considerable expansion to the west. The Tarim Basin came under its dominion and Sogdiana, Ferghana, Transoxiana, and Tukharistan were established as protectorates. Chinese cultural dominance extended into other areas such as southeast Asia and northeast, into the region of Korea and Japan. Camel caravans carried goods through central Asia westward to Persia. Goods were transported to India and the Persian Gulf by sea. After the mid-eighth century, a T'ang standoff with a Turkish/Arab coalition took place at Talas in Samarkand. This was a highwater mark for both sides. The result of their encounters was that the Chinese technology of paper making and printing was passed on to the West. This was just the beginning of what was to come.

The Islamic presence in central Asia was joined by Uighurs and Tibetans. Over the eighth and ninth centuries imperial authority was challenged by rebellion at the provincial level as well. Peasant rebellions and provincial autonomy destroyed the T'ang and after 907 China broke up into ten different states, which ushered in the era known as the Five Dynasties and Ten Kingdoms.

EXERCISE 19
T'ANG CHINA: UNITY AND EXPANSION, A.D. 618–907

I.   MAKING THE MAP

1.   Locate and label the Yellow Sea, the East China Sea, the South China Sea.
2.   Locate and label the Yellow River, the Yangtze River, the West (Hsi) River, the Aral Sea.
3.   Locate and label the Gobi Desert, the Himalaya Mountains, Korea (Silla), the Kunlun Mountains, the Pamir Mountains, the Tarim Basin.
4.   Locate and label Manchuria, Mongolia, Tibet, Japan.
5.   Locate with a black dot and label Loyang, Ch'ang-An, Nanking (Jianksang), Hangchou (Hangzhou), Peking (Beijing), Yang-chou (Yangzhou), Tun-huang (Dung-uang), Kashgar.
6.   Show the line of the "Silk Road."
7.   Show the line of the Grand Canal.
8.   Show the line of the Great Wall.

II.   READING THE MAP

1.   The Grand Canal connects the city of _____ with _____ to the south.
2.   The "Silk Road" ran in an _____ to _____ direction from the city of _____.
3.   The large natural border in the north of T'ang China beyond the Great Wall is the _____.
4.   At its greatest extent T'ang China measured approximately _____ miles from the East China Sea to the Aral Sea.

III.   UNDERSTANDING THE MAP

1.   Name the regions incorporated into T'ang China at its peak.
2.   T'ang expansion in central Asia was challenged by what elements in the mid eighth century?
3.   During the Sui and T'ang era the Grand Canal facilitated the development of what major region of China?
4.   How would you characterize the situation in northern China during the Period of Disunion (A.D. 206–581)?
5.   What combination of problems brought the Sui dynasty to an end?

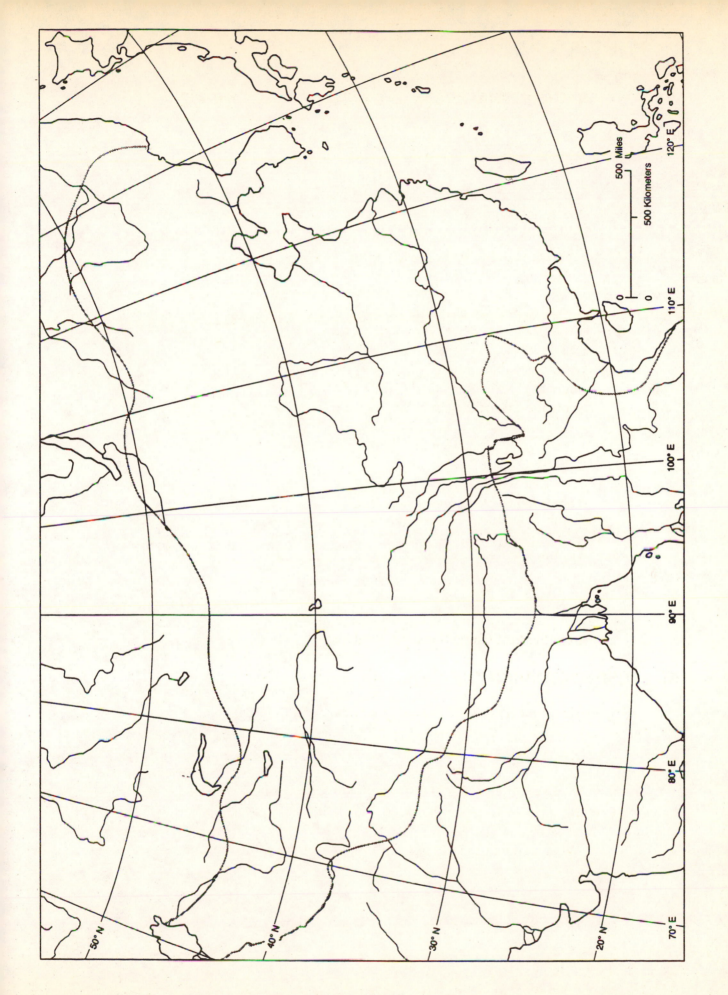

Exercise 19: T'ang China: Unity and Expansion, 618-907 A.D.

XX. POLITICAL REGIONALISM AND CULTURAL UNITY
IN THE GUPTA-HARSHA ERAS, A.D. 400–650

The end of the Mauryan Empire in the third century B.C. brought invaders to India. Greeks from Bactria and Parthia, along with nomads from Central Asia, moved into north and northwestern India. One group, the Kush, established an empire that stretched from the Sind beyond the Indus River east to Benares on the Ganges. Greeks and Scythians were able, in this era often called the "Dark Ages," to establish their dynasties and kingdoms in central and western India. This was a period in which there was considerable trade with the eastern Mediterranean and eventually Rome. Barbaricum, at the mouth of the Indus, and Barygaza to the south, at the head of the Gulf of Cambay, were major centers of this east-west trade across the Arabian Sea to the Persian Gulf and Red Sea. Taxila, on the upper Indus, became a major overland trading post through which silk from China passed on its way west.

The Guptas in Magadha, Tamils from Madras, and the Satavahanas in the Deccan are three examples of native dynasties which eventually emerged from the second through the sixth centuries. The Tamils controlled Ceylon and seaborne trade in that region. The Satavahana kingdom stretched from the mouth of the Godavan River to the shores of the Bay of Bengal, westward across the Deccan, nearly to the shores of the Arabian Sea by the mid-second century. It was bordered on the north by the Narmada River and the south by the Krishna. The Guptas from the Magadha governed from Pataliputra. Their territory extended from the area of Bengal west to the Punjab-Sind area, that is from the Ganges Delta to the Indus Delta. At its peak, this empire was focused on the semi-divine emperor who relied on tributary princes on the frontiers and semi-autonomous towns and villages in the interior. With the decline of the Roman Empire in the west, the trade relations of the Gupta shifted to southeast Asia. In the Gupta era the sciences, arts, and letters were promoted at the University at Nalanda. Many of the achievements in sculpture, architecture, Hinduism, and Buddhism had considerable impact in southeast Asia when transmitted there by merchants.

Dynastic quarrels and outside invaders brought an end to the Gupta Empire. The invasion of the White Huns (Nephalites) in the early sixth century also delivered a severe blow to the culture and economy of northern India. In the sixth century the later Gupta or Malwa Empire in west/central India flourished until replaced by the Kananj Empire led by Harsha (d. 648). Harsha's empire reached from Bengal at the Brahmaputra River mouth in the east to Gujerat, just east of the Indus River Delta. This would be the last empire in north India until the Mughal six hundred years later.

Under Harsha the authority in administrative and fiscal matters was delegated. His military campaigns created an empire which rivaled that of the Gupta but attempts at expansion south into the Deccan were blocked by the equally strong Chalukyas. Harsha's cosmopolitan regime fostered a remarkable flowering of the arts. Harsha's empire owed much to his personal abilities and on his death in 648 it fell apart.

Within a short time in the 750s Islamic invaders appeared in the Sind and succeeded in taking the city of Maltan. A second major wave would invade the region in the eleventh century. The Turkish founders of the Ghaznavid Empire opened several centuries of Moslem influence in northern India.

In the south three kingdoms, Chola, Pandijan, and Pallavan, continued under indigenous dynasties. Here, well protected by the Deccan Plateau, cultural traditions continued. The region was never unified, however, and never really free from factional conflict. The struggle for power did not hinder the lucrative economic connections in southeast Asia.

Time after time, events demonstrated that India was more open to and more vulnerable to aggressors from the west. To the north and east the Himalaya Mountains (the highest in the world), the Tibetan Plateau, and deserts proved effective barriers in or out. Consequently, Indian-Chinese contacts were limited. The route eastward through Burma and Southeast Asia up into China was every bit as difficult. The penetration of Buddhism from India to China was the significant exception to the general rule of limited contacts. There was very little cultural or economic influence by one on the other of these two populous and significant areas of the East.

EXERCISE 20
POLITICAL REGIONALISM AND CULTURAL UNITY IN THE
GUPTA-HARSHA ERAS, A.D. 400–650

I.   MAKING THE MAP

1,   Locate and label the Bay of Bengal, the Arabian Sea, the Indus River, the Ganges River, the Narbada River, the Godavari River.
2.   Locate and label the Himalaya Mountains, the Hindu Kush, Ceylon, the Great Indian Desert, the Deccan Plateau.
3.   Locate with a black dot and label Calcutta, Delhi, Pataliputra, Bombay, Ajanta.
4.   Locate and label Sind, Bengal, Maharashtra, Rajasthan, Chola.
5.   Locate and label Nepal, Afghanistan, Kashmir, Punjab.
6.   Show with a wide dark line the approximate boundaries of the Gupta Empire in the fifth century.

II.   READING THE MAP

1.   What is the approximate distance overland in miles from Bombay to Calcutta?
2.   What is the approximate distance overland in miles from Delhi to Calcutta?
3.   What was the major empire located to the northeast of India in the seventh and eighth centuries?

III.   UNDERSTANDING THE MAP

1.   What two regions outside India were important to cultural and economic development in the post-Mauryan and Gupta eras?
2.   In what region was the core of the Gupta Empire?
3.   What region of India was not controlled by the Gupta Empire?
4.   What important elements of Indian culture and religion were introduced to Southeast Asia during the Gupta era? By what means were these influences spread?
5.   What invaders destroyed Gupta rule and the urban cultural base in north India in the early sixth century?
6.   By what political and economic methods did Harsha temporarily unite north India in the seventh century?

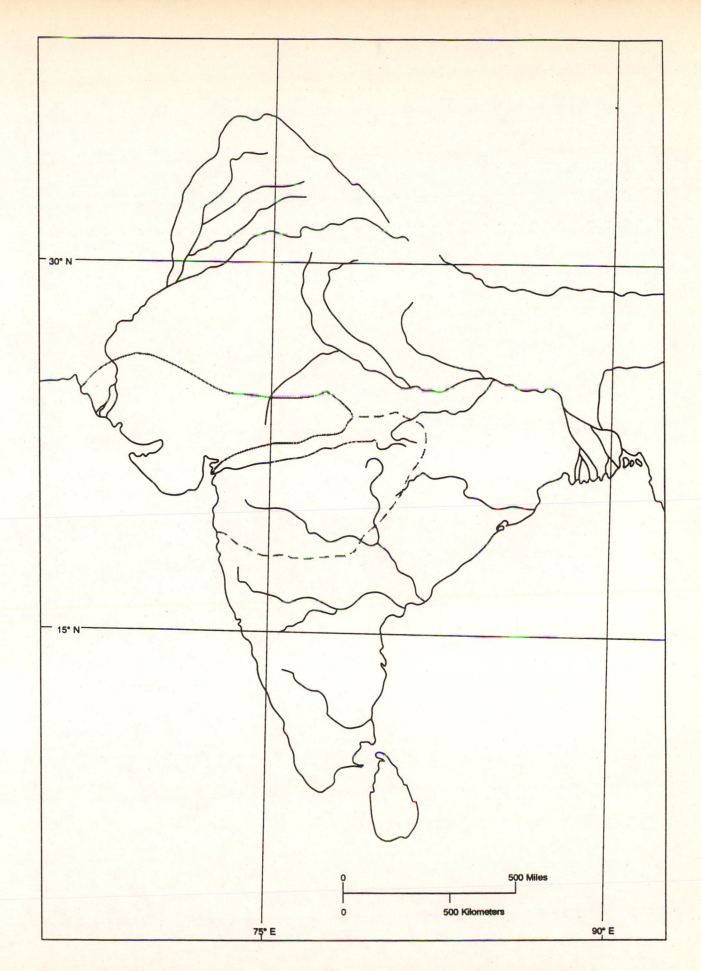

Exercise 20: Political Regionalism and Cultural Unity in the Gupta-Harsha Eras, 400–650 A.D.

XXI. SOUTHEAST ASIA, JAPAN AND KOREA

Southeast Asia, Japan, and Korea are geographically complex regions dominated by the Asian mainland and the Pacific and Indian oceans. The climate ranges from severe winter weather in northern Japan and Korea to extreme heat and humidity in the tropical south as far as Java. The terrain varies from extremely rugged mountains, many of which are volcanic, to impenetrably dense rain forests. Burma (Myanmar), Laos, Siam (Thailand), Cambodia, and Vietnam are in the peninsular region to the south of China.

Indonesia is a large complex of 13,667 islands which stretches east and west 3,200 miles across the south Pacific. Another group of over seven thousand islands, the Philippines, lies just to the north across the South China Sea from the mainland of Asia.

The Korean Peninsula is about four hundred miles long and lies on the northeast border of China due east of the Yellow Sea, Korea Bay, and the Gulf of Chihli. The Yalu River is the modern border between China and North Korea.

The Japanese islands are located directly northeast of Korea and the Chinese mainland. The northernmost of the three thousand islands is Hokkaido. The large island of Sakhalin, just beyond that, is claimed by Russia. Honshu, Shikoku, and Kyushu swing to the southeast to a point about 150 miles off the tip of South Korea at Pusan. The Sea of Japan separates the large central island of Honshu from the mainland some five hundred miles distant.

The long narrow nation of Vietnam has fourteen hundred miles of coastline. In the north, the main city is Haiphong, at the head of the Tonkin Gulf. In the south, Saigon is located at the eastern mouth of the Mekong River. Vietnam is cut off from the interior by mountains and dense forests. From the third century B.C. this region was dominated by China and eventually became a colony under the Han as Tonkin. Here, as elsewhere in Southeast Asia, the indigenous cultures mixed with the Chinese.

Khmer, or Cambodia, is an amorphous region about the size of Tennessee. It has largely been surrounded by its neighbors except for an opening in the south to the Gulf of Siam. The Khmer Kingdom of Angkor achieved a considerable measure of political, religious, and economic unity despite its lack of fixed borders from the ninth through the fourteenth centuries. Canals, reservoirs, and temple complexes brought prosperity and cultural development to the region. Angkor Wat and Angkor Boreii were important centers for Hindu influence from India.

Siam (Thailand), which runs north-south from the Gulf of Siam, was historically a major east-west crossroads region between China and India. Burma (Myanmar), lying to the northwest, is a Texas-sized region dominated by rugged mountains. Its major river system is the Irrawaddy to which runs south into the Bay of Bengal. Pagan was an important location in the dissemination of Buddhist influences in the region. Throughout this area Hindu-Buddhist influences, along with economic, political, and technical elements, made a significant impact through overseas trade.

In Java and Sumatra, as in Borneo, Cambodia, and Siam, there is ample evidence connected to the appearance of *Homo sapiens* (4000 B.C. in Java), and the eventual introduction of agriculture. Burials, tools and habitation sites show a progression through Bronze Age technology by at least 1000 B.C. and Iron Age by 500 B.C. Interaction in this crossroads area between the strong indigenous peoples and Chinese and Indian influences produced a variety of political, social, economic, and religious mixtures.

In Korea and Japan, an eclectic approach was taken by the native peoples as they responded to Chinese influence. Korea played a major role in the diffusion of culture to Japan. Chinese influence became important in the second century B.C. when a part of northern Korea became a commandery under the Han dynasty. In the third century there were three separate kingdoms in Korea: Koguryo in the north, Silla in the south, and Poekche in the southwest. In the seventh century Silla unified Korea with T'ang China's assistance. Its capital of Kyongju had a population of 700,000 and was a focal point for Chinese-Japanese trade. T'ang agricultural patterns and administrative methods were imported as well by Korea in this period.

In Japan many important early cultural and political influences came from the mainland. Immigrants entered the mainland from Korea and pushed the indigenous Ainu to the north. The political ideal of an imperial administration ruled by descendants of the Sun Goddess was established in the Yamato Era of the seventh century B.C. The Taika reform adapted from China in the seventh and eighth centuries A.D. represented an attempt to centralize the administration. In A.D. 710 a fixed single capital was established. It was modeled on Ch'ang-An of the T'ang dynasty and had a population of about 200,000. The Taika land and fiscal reforms proved to be unsuccessful in the long run, however. The mountainous nature of the islands made political unification difficult. Less than one-seventh of the land is arable. In the Heian period (794 to 1185) the capital was moved to Kyoto. In the four hundred years of this era, Japanese traditions counterbalanced the Chinese and Korean influences of the previous ages.

EXERCISE 21
SOUTHEAST ASIA, JAPAN, AND KOREA

I.   MAKING THE MAP

1.   Locate and label the South China Sea, the East China Sea, the Yellow Sea, the Sea of Japan.
2.   Locate and label the Yalu River, the Mekong River, the Irrawaddy River, the Straits of Tsushima.
3.   Locate and label the area of Burma, India, China, the Philippine Islands, Siam.
4.   Locate and label Khmer, Laos, Vietnam, Korea, Japan.
5.   Locate and label Kyoshu, Honshu, Hokkaido.
6.   Locate with a black dot and label Angkor, Canton, Hanoi, Bangkok, Mandalay, Pyongyang, Kaesong, Seoul, Nara, Kyoto, Edo.

II.   READING THE MAP

1.   Name the powerful nation that dominated the region of Vietnam politically and culturally from the second century B.C. as the province of Tonkin.
2.   The region west of Vietnam was dominated by the _____ Kingdom of _____.
3.   Another name for this region is _____.
4.   The major city in the north of Vietnam is _____.
5.   Name the three kingdoms of Korea.
6.   The largest of the Japanese Islands is _____.

III.   UNDERSTANDING THE MAP

1.   Name the major river and the direction of flow of the largest river system in the area of Vietnam and Cambodia.
2.   From what area did the major threat to the Korean Kingdom emerge?
3.   Which of the Korean kingdoms took the lead in unifying the peninsula and who was its ally in this achievement?
4.   What man-made improvements were vital to the success of the Khmer state?
5.   The earliest political organization in Japan was centered in what area?
6.   What were the names and locations of the earliest capitals of Japan?
7.   What is the name of the body of water separating Japan from Korea?
8.   What is the name of the river system at the north of the Korean Peninsula?
9.   If you were to travel directly east from Kyoto in Japan, at what area would you land in the United States?
10.   What is the approximate distance in miles between these areas?

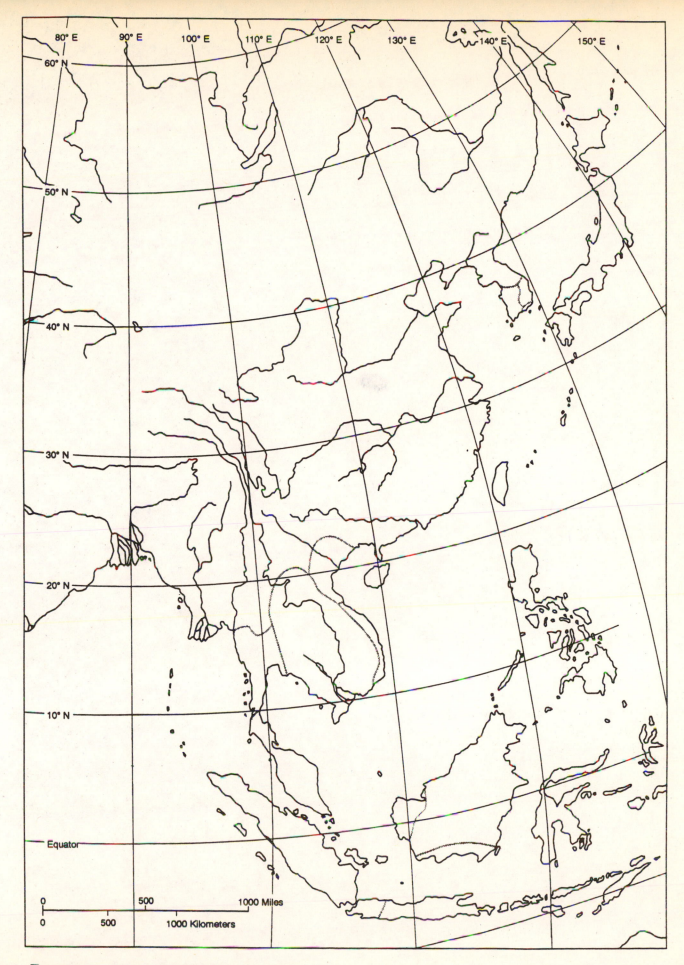

80° E 90° E 100° E 110° E 120° E 130° E 140° E 150° E
60° N
50° N
40° N
30° N
20° N
10° N
Equator

0 500 1000 Miles
0 500 1000 Kilometers

Exercise 21: Southeast Asia, Korea and Japan

97

XXII. THE CAROLINGIAN EMPIRE

The Germanic Franks settled in northern Europe between the Elbe and the Rhine on the shores of the North Sea in the latter half of the third century. From there they spread south and west in the fourth and fifth centuries to displace the Visigoths, the Kingdom of Syagrius, the Burgundians in Gaul, and the Ostrogothic remnants in Provence. Conquests under Clovis (d. 511) were matched by gains elsewhere such as against the Alamani and Thuringians east across the Rhine. Clovis's capital was at Paris on the Seine and he ruled with the support of Gallo-Romans, the hierarchy of the church and Frankish arms. His acceptance of Christianity from Rome gave him another weapon against other Arian-Christian Germanic groups. Austrasia was the eastern core area of Frankish land along with Neustria beyond the Loire River to the west. Over the course of the sixth century powerful families who had gained from supporting the Merovingians competed for control over royal power. This often bloody struggle for power resulted in the emergence of one family, that of Pepin of Herstal. Its strength was based in the region of Aachen about two hundred miles northeast of Paris toward the Rhine. Its victory against its Neustrian rivals was capped by virtual rule of the kingdom as "mayors of the palace."

Pepin's son, Charles Martel, earned considerable prestige by turning back a Moslem expeditionary force which had crossed the Pyrenees from Spain at Poitiers in 732. Pepin the Short, one of Charles's sons, deposed the last Merovingian king and made himself king of all the Franks in 751. The Papal Legate Boniface supported this settlement by anointing him as King. Frankish assistance in Italy against the Lombards resulted in the creation of the Papal States or the Donation of Pepin under the authority of the popes in Rome.

It was Charles, the surviving son of Pepin the Short, who assumed the burden of authority in 768. He took up the conquest and Christianization of the Saxons, a brutal process of over thirty years. The defeat of the Lombard Kingdom added those territories in northwestern Italy (774), and confirmed Frankish protection of the Papal States. The region of Bavaria was also incorporated into the realm in the following decade.

Territories at the head of the Adriatic: Friuli, Carinthia, and Ostrmark were organized as marches as was Pannonia, the Avar Kingdom to the east. A march was an area of nominal control which was a buffer state on the frontier. In the west the Breton March separated Neustria from the Brittany Peninsula. The Spanish March established the border between Gaul and Arab-controlled Spain at the end of the eighth century. The Kingdom of Asturias and the Basques continued as independent enclaves there. The British Isles were dominated by Celtic and Anglo-Saxon kingdoms.

Charles the Great (Charlemagne) was anointed emperor by Pope Leo III in A.D. 800. The East Roman Emperor in Constantinople continued to claim Sicily, southern Italy, Venetia, Istria, and Dalmatia. Cultural and religious unity were permanent achievements of the Carolingian Empire. Charles the Great's son, Louis the Pious, ruled in that tradition with the support of the educated hierarchy of the Church. Counts and dukes appointed by the king were responsible for urban, administrative, and frontier districts. Large tracts of land were given out to the aristocracy as rewards and inducements for loyalty to the royal government at Aachen. A blend of tradition and innovation resulted in agricultural productivity, stability, and population growth. The rural manors in the hands of the nobility replaced the towns as political and economic centers. In general, many peasants were reduced to serfdom and found themselves economically attached to the agricultural estate.

The successors of Charles the Great could not command the loyalty he had enjoyed. They followed the Frankish pattern of dividing up the realm among their sons in a futile attempt to bring harmony and administrative efficiency. Ultimately, these substantially weaker kings lost authority to powerful men of the realm and were unable to defend the empire against Germanic invaders from the North, central Asian Magyars from the east, and renewed Arab incursions from the south.

EXERCISE 22
THE CAROLINGIAN EMPIRE

I. MAKING THE MAP

1. Locate and label the Atlantic Ocean, the Mediterranean Sea, the North Sea.
2. Locate and label the Rhine River, the Seine River, the Loire River, the Danube River.
3. Locate and label the British Isles, Italy, Asturias, Anatolia, Brittany, Sicily.
4. Locate with a black dot and label Rome, Ravenna, Constantinople, Toledo, Barcelona, Aix-la-Chapelle (Aachen), Verdun, Tours, Lyon, Cordova.
5. Show the boundary line of the Carolingian Empire as of A.D. 814.
6. Show the area of the Pyrenees Mountains, the Alps.
7. Show in red the European areas of the Byzantine Empire *ca.* A.D. 800.

II. READING THE MAP

1. In the time of Charlemagne, the _____ had replaced the _____ as the dominant power in Spain.
2. The approximate distance in miles from Rome to Aix-la-Chapelle is _____.
3. Name the major enemy faced by the Carolingians to their north across the Rhine River.
4. Central Italy in the era of the Carolingians was organized as _____ and administered from _____.
5. The capital of Charlemagne's empire was located at _____.

III. UNDERSTANDING THE MAP

1. Name the new elements in Eastern Europe which challenged the power of the Byzantine Empire.
2. By what administrative means did Charlemagne organize the eastern borders of his empire?
3. What Germanic kingdom did the Carolingians displace in northern Italy ?
4. What peoples made up the major power in the British Isles during the seventh and eighth centuries?
5. What were the component parts of the Carolingian Empire after Charlemagne's death?

Exercise 22: The Carolingian Empire

Map labels:
- 20° W
- 10° W
- 0°
- 10° E
- 20° E
- 30° E
- 40° E
- 50° E
- 50° N
- 40° N
- 30° N

Scale:
- 0 — 500 Miles
- 0 — 500 Kilometers

XXIII. NEW FORMATIONS IN EUROPE: SAXONS, SLAVS, MAGYARS, VIKINGS, AND SARACENS

In the eighth, ninth, and tenth centuries migrants, invaders, and raiders from the north and east ranged through Europe from Russia to the Atlantic and beyond. In addition, new waves of Arabs made their way across the Mediterranean from North Africa into southern Europe. Germanic Angles and Saxons had been established in the British Isles since the fifth century. In the eighth and ninth centuries, Northmen crossed the North Sea from Denmark and Norway to raid and settle in Britain, Ireland, and the smaller islands off Scotland. Normans would raid the British Isles, settle in western France and Britain, range into the Mediterranean, and from their kingdom in south Italy launch attacks against the Byzantine Empire. Swedes made their way across the Baltic, established a center at Novgorod, and moved south down the Dnieper to Kiev and across the Black Sea to attack Constantinople in the tenth century.

Prior to that time, in the fifth, sixth, and seventh centuries, West Slavs (Poles, Czechs, Slovaks), South Slavs (Croats, Slovenes, Serbs), and East Slavs (Russians) and Ukrainians had moved into eastern and southeastern Europe. They were settled into this vast area from the Baltic beyond the Don River to the Caspian Sea in the east. To the south, they reached the Danube River, the Carpathian Mountains, and the Balkan Ranges on to the shores of the Black Sea, the Aegean and the Adriatic. Into this mixture first came the central Asian Bulgars and then the Magyars. This was a period of great turmoil which resulted in the collapse of some kingdoms and empires and the creation of new ones. In certain cases new states were created as a response to the invaders, and in other cases the invaders themselves created new states.

The Carolingian Empire, in the west, is a significant example of the collapse of a major state. On the eastern frontiers of Europe, the Byzantine Empire took major losses in Greece, the Mediterranean and in the Danube provinces, but survived. In the British Isles, the variety of smaller kingdoms came to be replaced by Danes and in the eleventh century by branches of the Normans who had recently consolidated their territories in Normandy in western France. In Russia, Northmen (Swedes) stimulated the creation of a state first at Novgorod and then farther south at Kiev. Important cultural and religious contacts were established with Byzantium after futile attacks against Constantinople. Kievan princes had continued difficulty holding their own against barbarian groups such as the Pechenegs. Elsewhere in southern and eastern Europe the Serbs, Croatians, Slavicized Bulgars, and central Asian Magyars began the process of transformation by carving out independent kingdoms. Opportunity and circumstance dictated their eventual east or west orientation in the tenth and eleventh centuries.

In central Europe the Saxons, led by Henry I and Otto the Great in the tenth century, controlled much of the eastern two-thirds of the Carolingian Empire and held off the Slavs, Magyars, and Arabs. These achievements and agreements with the church gave Otto the crown of the Holy Roman Empire in 962. Control over his powerful dukes and a loyal army allowed Otto and his successors to forestall the worst effects of the feudalism which dismembered the west. The relationship with the church hierarchy originally contributed to fiscal stability until quarrels with the papacy disrupted that delicate balance. The Saxon/Ottonian attempts to revive the Roman Empire with the capital at Rome resulted in a costly and futile commitment to Italy. Saracen Arabs launched seaborne attacks from North Africa and took Sicily, Corsica and Sardinia, and southern Italy in the ninth and tenth centuries. In the ninth century, southern Italy, Rome, and southern Gaul were often at their mercy.

One branch of the Normans that had settled in Normandy invaded the British Isles and dominated the Saxons there. Others ended Byzantine rule in south Italy and forced the Arabs out of Sicily. Palermo became the capital of a United Kingdom including Apulia, Calabria, and Sicily, which challenged the papacy and invaded Byzantine Greece. Piracy was often rampant throughout the western Mediterranean. Eventually, the Byzantine fleet and the Normans forced the Saracens out of the region.

It was the Mongol, Genghis Khan (d. 1227) in the Far East, who built a large territorial empire that reached from the Pacific to eastern Europe. Mongol armies ended Kievan power following Cuman and Pecheneg activities in the region in the twelfth century. By the thirteenth century the Mongol Empire was the largest the world had ever seen. Their brutal tactics took the Mongols into Poland, Bohemia, Moravia, and Hungary. They ruled their western lands from Sarai on the Volga. Under Kubla Khan in the late thirteenth century, they controlled Persia as well.

EXERCISE 23
NEW FORMATIONS IN EUROPE: SAXONS, SLAVS, MAGYARS, VIKINGS, AND SARACENS

I. **MAKING THE MAP**

1. Locate and label the Atlantic Ocean, the North Sea, the Mediterranean Sea, the Black Sea, the Baltic Sea.
2. Locate and label the Danube River, the Volga River, the Dnieper River, the Rhine River, the Rhone River, the Vistula River.
3. Locate with a black dot and label Rome, Venice, Constantinople, Cadiz, Barcelona, Marseilles, Tunis, Tripoli, Aachen, Kiev, Novgorod.
4. Show in red outline the area of the empire of Otto the Great.
5. Show the area of the original Viking homeland.
6. Show the approximate area of settlement of the Magyars.
7. Locate and label the approximate area of Croatia and Serbia as of A.D. 1000.
8. Locate and label Normandy.

II. **READING THE MAP**

1. What is the approximate distance in miles from Novgorod to Kiev?
2. What is the approximate distance in miles from Kiev to Constantinople?
3. From what areas did the Arabs launch their campaigns against Europe in the ninth century?
4. By what means and from what general direction did the Vikings attack Constantinople?
5. In what areas of western Europe did Vikings succeed in establishing themselves?
6. What was the approximate origin of the Magyar invaders?

III. **UNDERSTANDING THE MAP**

1. What region of Europe was best able to withstand the invasions of the eighth through the tenth centuries?
2. What was the fate of the western half of the Carolingian Empire in the ninth and tenth centuries?
3. What was the main area of settlement of the South Slavs?
4. Name the new kingdom that emerged in Eastern Europe north of the Danube and west of the Carpathian Mountains.
5. What new state emerged south of the Danube comprised of a mixture of Slavs and central Asians?
6. As successors to the Carolingians, the Saxons under Otto the Great and the Salians were committed to what territory to their south?

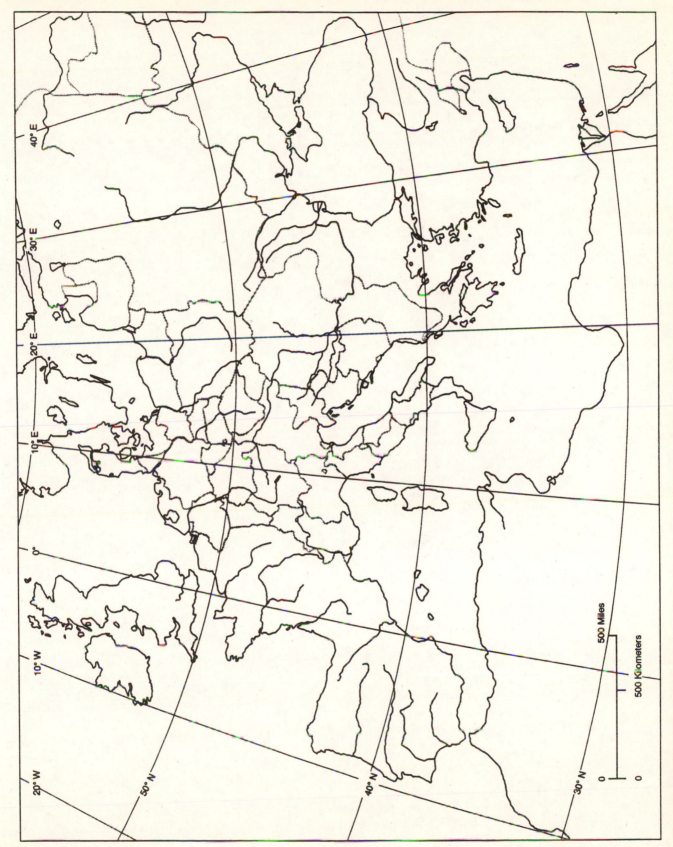

Exercise 23: New Formations in Europe, East and West: Saxons, Slavs, Magyars and Saracens

500 Miles

500 Kilometers

109

XXIV. THE EARLY MIDDLE AGES: EMPERORS, KINGS, AND CRUSADERS, A.D. 1000–1300

Dramatic transformations took place throughout Europe and the Middle East in the period from the tenth through the thirteenth centuries. Ancient empires found themselves threatened, some proved capable of revitalization, and new empires were created. A variety of new kingdoms appeared in the west and in the eastern lands of Europe. Central Asian barbarian groups had a long-term impact on Eastern Europe as well.

The Norman dukes who had established their power in western France ventured into new areas in the eleventh century. Under William the Conqueror, Norman-French feudalism was transplanted to the British Isles. The Normans controlled the Crown and dispossessed the Anglo-Saxon aristocracy there. William's great-grandson, Henry II (d. 1189), made himself master of the Angevin Empire, which included substantial continental holdings. By inheritance and marriage he controlled Normandy, Maine, Touraine, Anjou, Aquitaine and Poitou, virtually one half of France. Future generations were taken up with the struggle over power between kings and feudal lords which was further complicated by friction with the authority of the Church.

The struggle over power on the part of these monarchs involved continental territorial ambitions and challenging fiscal demands. Under Edward I (d. 1307), the Crown annexed Wales but was less successful in Scotland. In the fourteenth century, territorial and dynastic claims on the continent would involve England in the Hundred Years War (1337–1453). In France, from the crowning of Hugh Capet, French kings had a continued struggle with royal authority, expanding the royal domain and achieving national integrity. Royal prestige and power was enhanced under Philip II (d. 1223) and Philip IV (d. 1314) through administrative and fiscal reform. French national unity prevailed in support of the monarchy in the fiscal quarrels with the papacy in Rome.

In Spain, the Reconquista was a war of liberation that began in the ninth century. A three-centuries-long struggle resulted in the Moslem confinement to the area of Granada in the southern part of the Spanish Peninsula. Four kingdoms emerged: Aragon, Castile, Portugal, and Navarre. Crusading zeal turned this effort into a Holy War against Moslems and Jews.
In the eleventh century, the Byzantine Empire had hardly settled affairs in the Balkans with the defeat of the Bulgars when it was forced to confront another serious threat. Weak leadership and a struggle between the imperial bureaucracy and the landed aristocracy made the empire vulnerable to central Asian invaders. Seljuk Turks defeated Byzantine armies and overran the vital regions of Armenia and Anatolia.

At the same time Venetians and Normans posed an equally serious threat from the west. Venice and other powerful urban centers in Italy had come to be serious economic competitors in the central and eastern Mediterranean. The Normans had put an end to Byzantine power in south Italy and Arab power in Sicily. In the twelfth century, Normans united Sicily, Calabria, and Apulia. They also launched attacks against Byzantium. The western response to Constantinople's request for warriors did not result in the restoration of the Byzantine Empire or the demise of Islam. Neither the Crusader Kingdoms in Syria and Palestine nor the Latin Empire created after the Fourth Crusade (1204) could sustain themselves. The Turks, even though temporarily diverted from their objectives by the Mongol advance, proved persistently aggressive.

Elsewhere in Eastern Europe, the Bulgarian threat revived in the Second Greater Bulgarian Empire. A Hungarian Kingdom was established beginning with Stephen I (d. 1038). It stretched from the Carpathians and Transylvania in the east to Moravia and Austria in the west. It also extended south into Croatia.

Central Europe and Germany took an alternative path in the tenth century. Under the Saxons, Salians, and Hohenstaufens, the Holy Roman Empire was the dominant ideal of political organization. From Henry the Fowler (d. 936) to Frederick II (d. 1273), hostile elements such as the Magyars and Saracens were defeated. These emperors had to contend with challenges from feudal barons and princes at home and an aggressive Reform Papacy in Italy. Ultimately, Germany would see neither a strong empire, a strong state, nor strong kings.

EXERCISE 24
THE EARLY MIDDLE AGES: EMPERORS, KINGS, AND CRUSADERS, A.D. 1000–1300

I.   MAKING THE MAP

1.   Locate and label the Atlantic Ocean, the Black Sea, the Mediterranean Sea, the English Channel, the Aegean Sea, the Sea of Marmara, the Hellespont.
2.   Locate and label the Rhine River, the Danube River, the Volga River, the Nile River.
3.   Locate and label Cyprus, Rhodes, Malta.
4.   Locate and label the area of the British Isles, France, Spain, the Papal States, Egypt, the Byzantine Empire *ca.* 1095.
5.   Locate with a black dot and label Moscow, Kiev, Constantinople, Jerusalem, Damascus, Antioch, Avignon, Rome, Venice, Palermo, Barcelona, Edessa, Cordova, Seville, Granada, Toledo, Marseilles, Manzikert, Nicaea.
7.   Locate and label the area of Normandy, the Kingdom of Leon and Castile, Poland, Hungary, Rus, Aragon, the Crusader States, the Latin Kingdom.

II.   READING THE MAP

1.   Name the areas where the Normans were successful in establishing themselves in Europe.
2.   The Anatolian territories of the Byzantine Empire were overrun by the _____ who originated in _____ in the eleventh century.
3.   Eastern Europe between the Holy Roman Empire and the Byzantine Empire was transformed by the development of such states as _____, _____, _____, and _____.
4.   The Crusader States were established in the area of the _____ Mediterranean from just north of _____ and south beyond _____.
5.   The Latin Empire of 1214 was built on the remnants of the _____ Empire located in _____ and a narrow strip of territory on the shores of the _____.
6.   The only region in the south of Spain to resist reconquest was _____.

III.   UNDERSTANDING THE MAP

1.   In addition to the Turks what other major threat did Eastern Europe face from Asia?
2.   What elements challenged the Byzantine Empire from the west in the twelfth and thirteenth centuries?

3. In what western region were the Crusaders against Islam more successful in the long run?

4. English kings of the thirteenth and fourteenth centuries were preoccupied with control of what territories in the British Isles?

5. In addition to competition from their vassals, the kings of France in the twelfth and thirteenth centuries had to deal with the claims of what other monarchs and their territory?

6. Name the three powers that had territorial claims in Italy in the twelfth and thirteenth centuries.

7. The Holy Roman Emperors from Otto the Great to Frederick Barbarossa were continually preoccupied with incorporating what territories to their south into a restored Roman Empire?

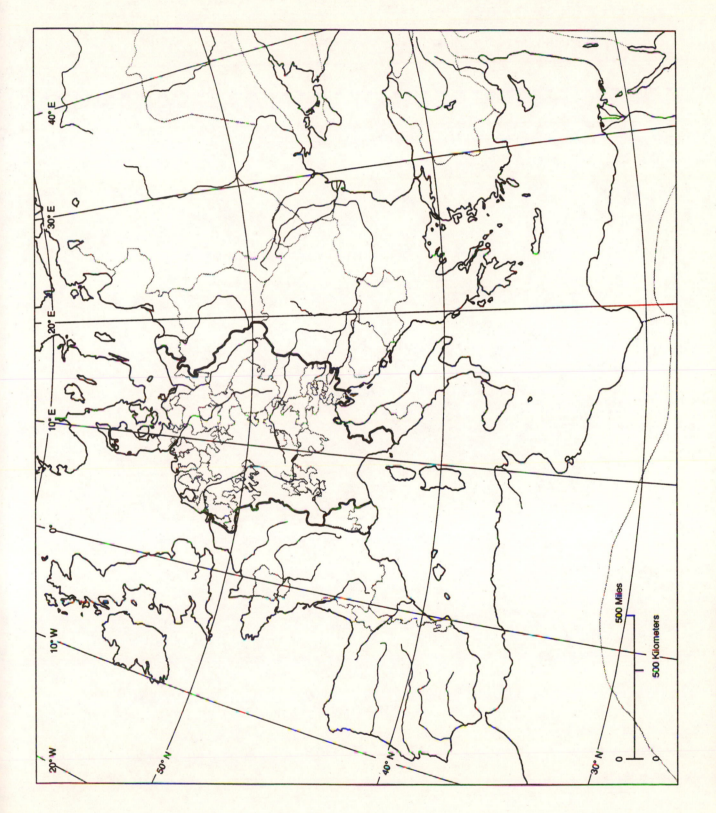

Exercise 24: The Early Middle Ages: Emperors, Kings and Crusaders, 1000-1300 A.D.

XXV. THE HIGH MIDDLE AGES: KINGDOMS AND EMPIRES, 1200–1500

The fourteenth and fifteenth centuries were critical in European political development. In the West, England, France, and Spain emerged from serious trials with centralized monarchies and well-defined territorial horizons. Central Europe was unable or unwilling to create a centralized state. Outside Germany, the Habsburgs created a dynastic empire. It was greater than any other in Europe and eventually included territories in the New World as well. For different reasons, Italy also remained divided. To the east, the conquest of the Byzantine Empire by the Turks would alter the scene in southeast Europe for centuries. Dynastic disputes and other challenges to royal authority kept Hungary and Poland from uniting effectively. Muscovy was an exception in the East, where a strong absolutist state centered on Moscow eventually emerged when Mongol power began to recede.

Over the course of the fourteenth and fifteenth centuries, the English and French were at war on the continent and fought civil wars at home. English and French kings took their people to war over dynastic and territorial claims that went back to the Norman Conquest. Each side felt compelled to defend, expand, or recover claims of French territory from Flanders to Aquitaine. Ultimately, the English withdrew from the continent but French kings faced an equally formidable enemy in the ambitious Duke of Burgundy, who succeeded in temporarily creating a large and powerful state within a state. In the latter half of the fifteenth century, English monarchs faced similar challenges from their feudal aristocracy in the War of the Roses. Henry Tudor's victory paved the way for centralized monarchy.

The diverse regions and elements of the Spanish Peninsula were brought together at the close of the fifteenth century through the dual monarchy of Ferdinand and Isabella. The long tradition of national and religious crusade put an end to Islamic resistance when the Kingdom of Granada was incorporated into the unified Kingdom of Castile and Aragon. The separate Kingdom of Portugal was located on the west coast along the Atlantic. The Aragonese, long oriented to the Mediterranean, also controlled Sardinia, Sicily, and southern Italy by the mid fifteenth century.

In Germany, no centralized territorial state emerged. Instead, there were hundreds of separate principalities, kingdoms, and duchies. Autonomy was recognized by the "Golden Bull" of 1356. The Holy Roman Empire was effectively dismantled but the title continued to carry prestige. It remained for the Habsburgs to build a new empire through dynastic marriage and diplomacy. Under Charles V (d.1556), this empire would include Austria, the Low Countries, Spain, The Kingdom of Naples and Sicily, and Spanish territories in the New World.

Italy was a divided and much fought over area in this period. In the north lay the city-states, duchies, and republics such as Florence, Milan, Pisa, Genoa, and Venice. Central Italy was ruled from Rome as the Papal States. The Avignon Papacy and the Great Schism severely curtailed the secular power of the popes. The Angevin French and Spanish Aragonese fought over their claims in southern Italy and Sicily as well.

The most dramatic change in the East was the success of the Turkish conquest of the Byzantine Empire. These nomadic warriors had converted to Islam in their westward sweep which would eventually take them to the gates of Vienna. They would be a permanent presence in Eastern Europe when they overran Bulgaria, Serbia, Croatia, and eventually, Hungary. Ivan the Great (d. 1505) capitalized on a growing spiritual and national movement to begin a strong state in Russia. He saw himself as the successor of the Byzantine emperors and Moscow as the new center of Eastern Orthodox Christianity. He tamed the nobility and expanded the area he controlled to the west and north.

EXERCISE 25
THE HIGH MIDDLE AGES: KINGDOMS AND EMPIRES, 1200–1500

I.   MAKING THE MAP

    1.   Locate and label the Atlantic Ocean, the Black Sea, the Mediterranean Sea, the Bay of Biscay.

    2.   Locate and label the English Channel, the Hellespont, the Strait of Gibraltar, the Rhine River, the Danube River, the Vistula River, the Volga River.

    3.   Locate and label Ireland, Scotland, Poland, Lithuania, Hungary, Poland, Bohemia, Austria, Spain.

    4.   Locate and color in red the Papal States.

    5.   Locate and label Moldavia and the Crimean Khanate.

    6   Color in blue the European area of the Ottoman Empire, in green the Venetian Republic and in yellow the Kingdom of the Two Sicilies.

    7.   Show in orange the area of Burgundy, Aquitaine, Normandy, Gascony, Brittany.

    8.   Locate with a black dot and label Rome, Istanbul, Venice, Paris, London, Vienna, Barcelona, Warsaw.

    (Duplicate the blank map to complete 4-7).

II.   READING THE MAP

    1.   The areas of Spain united by Ferdinand and Isabella by 1500 were _____, _____, and _____.

    2.   The two leading cities of Poland are _____ and _____ on the _____ River.

    3.   English-French rivalry in the fourteenth and fifteenth centuries were centered on English claims in areas such as _____, _____, _____, and _____.

    4.   The region to the north of England which consistently resisted conquest was _____.

    5.   The Hundred Years War essentially ended the English monarchy's territorial claims in _____.

    6.   In the fourteenth century, an important area of German influence among the Slavic peoples on the Baltic Sea was _____.

    7.   The advances of the Ottoman Empire in Europe were counterbalanced by Islamic losses in _____.

III.   UNDERSTANDING THE MAP

    1.   Name the most powerful empire in Europe in the last half of the fifteenth century.

    2.   In what areas of Western Europe did new territorial and political systems emerge in the fifteenth and sixteenth centuries?

    3.   How would you characterize the political patterns of the Holy Roman Empire after the mid fourteenth century?

    4.   Name the important Habsburg dominions in Europe as of 1500.

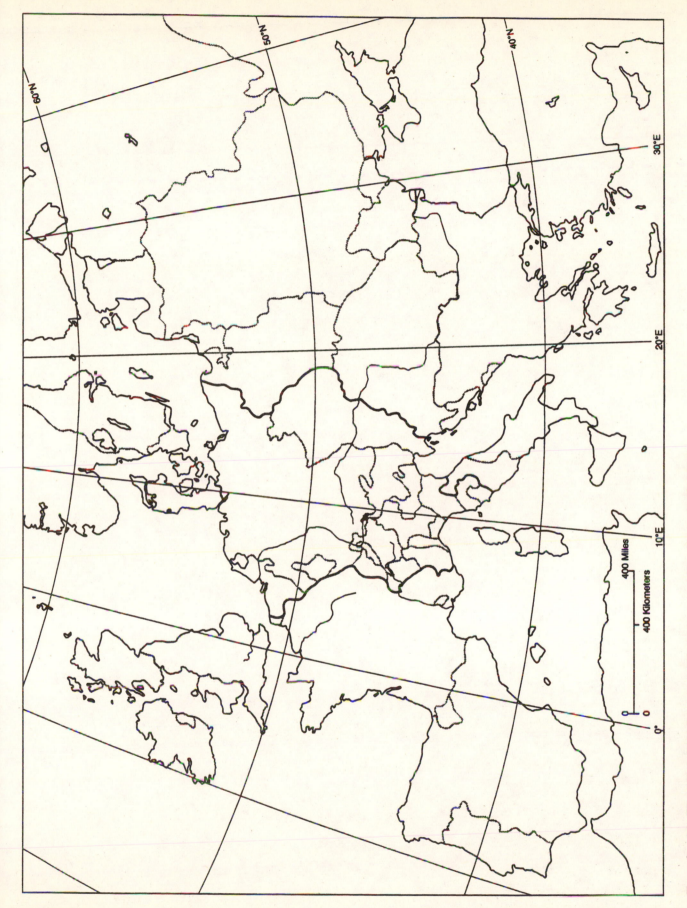

Exercise 25: The High Middle Ages: Kingdoms and Empires, 1200–1500

400 Miles

400 Kilometers

XXVI. SUNG (SONG) CHINA, THE MONGOLS, MING CHINA, AND IMPERIAL JAPAN

The period from 1000 to about 1600 brought profound transformations in east Asia. In China the Sung dynasty's (960–1279) achievements were balanced against the Mongol conquest until indigenous rule was restored in the Ming in the fourteenth century. In Japan, the struggle for political unity took place during the Kamakura and Ashikaga shogunates. In Japan and Korea distinctive patterns emerged with continued influences from the mainland.

Sung China was continually troubled with restless barbarians on its northern frontier. In the early twelfth century, the Jurchen took northern China and by the end of the thirteenth century the Mongols took all of China. With the Jurchen conquest, the Sung capital of Kaifeng fell and a new government was established at Hangchou. Prior to its collapse, the Sung gave up the costly efforts to control the frontier areas of Sinkiang, Tibet, Mongolia, Manchuria, and Vietnam. Instead, the capital at Kaifeng controlled the area of the Han, south of the Great Wall. This city of about one million was located on the Grand Canal and served as an administrative, commercial, and manufacturing center. Its location was ideal to draw on the southern agricultural areas. With the use of coal as fuel, China produced an abundance of iron and steel goods. The population of Sung China has been estimated at one hundred million.

When the northern barbarian group, the Jurchen, turned on the Sung and the north was lost after 1127, a new capital was built at the mouth of the Yangtze. From Hangchou, the Southern Sung flourished for another century until the Mongol conquest. During this era, efforts were concentrated on sea commerce in Southeast Asia and India. An elaborate system of canals and river channels in the Yangtze and Canton deltas enhanced this overseas trade. Hangchou, with a population of a million and a half, was the largest of numerous cities including Soochow. Foochow, in the south of China, flourished as a great international center.

It was the grandson of Genghis Khan, Kublai Khan, who completed the conquest of China in 1279. His capital was at Peking and from there Korea and northern Vietnam were conquered. Neighboring areas became tribute territories. Mobility and military terror combined to build an empire that stretched from the Pacific into the heart of Eastern Europe. The Mongol era in China is called the Yuan and utilized well-established Chinese administrative systems. Kublai was a demanding but capable ruler. China was the center of his empire and Peking the capital. The trade and communicative networks were restored and a measure of stability was re-established. Chinese resentment of foreign rule erupted under the less competent successors of Kublai and a new dynasty, the Ming, drove the Mongols out of China in the later fourteenth century.

The Ming dynasty restored Chinese integrity, albeit with a heavy hand. Its ideal was that of a solid, productive agricultural society. Production was increased in a diversified system which produced staples and cash crops in abundance. In the sixteenth century the introduction of New World crops, such as corn, potatoes, and peanuts, contributed to the nutritional base of the Chinese diet. Ming maritime activity was designed to reflect their power and prestige. Ming voyages to Southeast Asia, India, the Persian Gulf and East Africa on large ships, while impressive, had little long-run impact. Ming emperors ruled, from Peking, utilizing an extensive tributary system that included Korea, Tibet, Vietnam, Indonesia, and the Philippines.

The Japanese islands in the period from the twelfth through the sixteenth centuries were troubled by dissension and warfare. Though successful in turning back Mongol invasions in the thirteenth century, Japan did not develop a centrally organized administration until the seventeenth century. Localized patterns of defense and administration were characteristic of the Kamakura era. There was a nominal emperor in Kyoto and a shogunate power in Kamakura. Actual administration was conducted by methods roughly similar to those of Western feudalism which were based on lord–vassals relationships. Political turmoil continued under the Ashikaja Shogunate and intensified in the fifteenth century. The capital at Kyoto was destroyed and clan rivalry and civil war prevailed until much of Japan was unifed by Hideyoshi in the 1590s. Ironically, cultural elements advanced and the economy flourished in this era. Urban areas grew and towns connected to feudal castles came to be important. Japanese ships were active in a mix of commerce and piracy with the mainland. Korea was particularly vulnerable to Japanese raids in search of grain and slaves.

EXERCISE 26
SUNG (SONG) CHINA, THE MONGOLS, MING CHINA, AND IMPERIAL JAPAN

I. MAKING THE MAP

1. Locate and label the Pacific Ocean, the Sea of Japan, the Yellow Sea, the East China Sea, the South China Sea.

2. Locate and label the Yellow River, the Yangtze River, the Indus River, the Bramaputra River.

3. Locate and label the Persian Gulf, the Arabian Sea, the Caspian Sea, the Indian Ocean, the Bay of Bengal.

4. Locate and label Mongolia, Japan, India, Persia, Arabia, Tibet, Russia, Anam, Korea, the Tsushima Straits.

5. Locate with a black dot and label Chengdu, Kaifeng, Lin'an (Hanzhou), Karakorum, Peking (Beijing), Ch'uan-chou (Quanghou), Foochow (Fujhou), Lhasa, Samarkand, Ormuz, Calcutta, Jidda, Mogadishu.

6. Locate with a black dot and label Kamakura, Kyoto, Nara, Osaka.

7. Show in red the area of Sung (Song) dynasty China. Draw a line showing the northern boundary of the Southern Sung (Song) territory.

8. Show by a thick, dark line the frontiers of the Mongol Empire at its greatest extent.

   (Duplicate the blank map to complete 8 and 9.)

II. READING THE MAP

1. In the eleventh century the region that posed a major problem to the Sung (Song), was the _____ Empire, located to the _____.

2. The capital of the Sung (Song) was at _____ and under the Southern Sung it was located at _____, also called _____.

3. In the twelfth century, the barbarian _____ founded the _____ dynasty and overwhelmed the Sung.

4. Internal commerce flourished during the Sung era (960–1279) through _____ transport over _____ and _____.

5. What is the approximate distance in miles overland between Karakorum and Kiev?

6. What city became the new capital of the Mongol Empire under Kublai Khan?

7. In the thirteenth century, Mongol expansion to the east was successful in _____ but failed in efforts to conquer _____.

8. Chinese voyages under the Ming in the _____ century went to Ormuz in the _____ Gulf, Jidda on the _____ Sea, and to Mogadishu on the coast of _____.

III.   UNDERSTANDING THE MAP

1.   In what regions of Japan were the major concentrations of population and why?
2.   Mongol conquest in Eastern Europe disrupted the development of what emerging state?
3.   In what regions did China traditionally face the greatest threat to independence and security?
4.   Name the most important such groups during the period from the tenth through the sixteenth centuries.
5.   How did maritime activity in the Ming dynasty differ from that in the Sung?
6.   Name the region in south Asia where the Mongols failed in conquest.

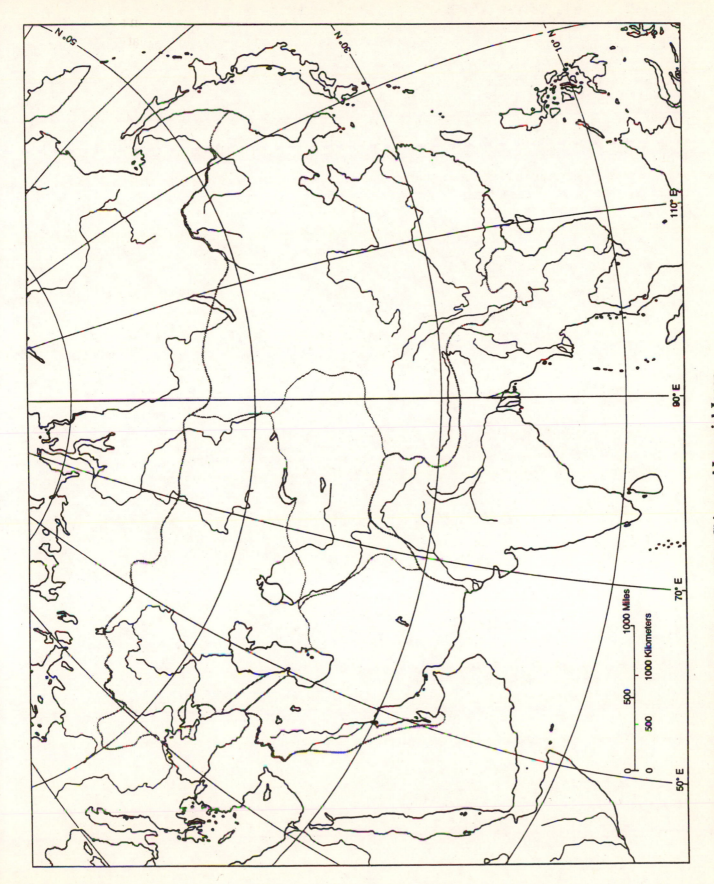

50° N

30° N

10° N

110° E

90° E

70° E

50° E

1000 Miles

1000 Kilometers

500

500

0

0

Exercise 26: Sung (Song) China, the Mongols, Ming China, and Imperial Japan

127

XXVII. RENAISSANCE ITALY: 1400–1600

In the fifteenth century, the Italian Peninsula was caught up in a continual struggle for power, glory, and wealth. In the north, duchies, principalities, republics, and city-states struggled to survive and grow at the expense of their neighbors. The Papal States in central Italy were governed from Rome and various popes sought secular powers in addition to their spiritual authority. To the south, the Kingdom of Naples, which usually included Sicily, was dominated by one or another continental monarch. To the east of Europe lay the besieged and weakened Byzantine Empire. In the same regions lay the growing threat of the Ottoman Turks. The newly emerged national monarchies in Spain, France, and England were the major powers in Western continental Europe. Swiss and German cities prospered with great mercantile potential in the north. Timing, geography, and enterprise came together in an era of unusual opportunity. Secular values and innovative economic developments combined in a new age of political and cultural advancement.

Northern Italy had long been free of the Holy Roman Empire and the feudal and dynastic struggles that beset Western Europe. A new vigorous urban based political and economic vision emerged here. The landlocked Duchy of Milan in Lombardy capitalized on Swiss and German commercial and banking opportunities. Genoa, at the head of the Tyrrhennian Sea, looked to the western Mediterranean and eventually beyond for markets. Florence, on the Arno River, became a great banking, manufacturing, and cultural center. Its control of Pisa, to the west, gave it access to the sea in competition with the Byzantine Empire. When challenged by the presence of the Ottoman Turks, Venice turned her state capitalism to expansion on land. These so-called city-states often came to be small-scale territorial states caught up in continual competition. Economic warfare was often combined with conflict on the battlefield where highly trained mercenary troops might replace complicated diplomatic maneuvering. These rich urban centers were protected by scientifically designed fortifications in response to the increasingly refined technology of artillery.

In one form or another, the cities of north Italy developed efficient productive systems of government and mercantile activity. New banking, manufacturing, and distribution methods applied in old and new markets had direct and long-lasting benefits. Venetian and Florentine trade networks reached into northern Europe to compete with the German economic activity there. The Medici family in Florence enhanced its wealth from cloth production with other commercial and banking enterprises. They combined political and financial power to lessen the possibility of bankruptcy with risky loans to kings or popes. Capital investment and money lending opportunities enabled successful new urban aristocrats to patronize arts and letters on an unprecedented level. The Papal States under the Pope's dominion exercised little real political authority, though Bologna, Ferrara, and Urbino might come into their orbit and an occasional pope was known to lead his own troops on the field of battle. The Kingdom of Naples was a real anomaly in a dynamic period of change. Naples, South Italy, and Sicily were claimed by both French and Aragonese monarchs. Naples flourished economically in the commerce between Italy and Spain. In the end, much of Italy would become a battleground in French and Spanish conflicts. Milan invited France to support it in a quarrel with Naples. Spain was then brought in at the request of other city-states which resulted in disastrous complications. In succeeding generations, Italian fortunes would decline, Italy would be at the mercy of Western monarchies and threatened by the Ottoman Turks from the East. A few enterprising Italians would, however, look beyond the Mediterranean and Europe for new opportunities.

EXERCISE 27
RENAISSANCE ITALY: 1400–1600

I.   **MAKING THE MAP**

1.   Locate and label the Atlantic Ocean, the Mediterranean Sea, the Black Sea, the Adriatic Sea.
2.   Locate and label the Po River, the Danube River, the Arno River, the Rhine River.
3.   Locate and label the Apennine Mountains, the Alps, the Pyrenees Mountains.
4.   Locate and label Spain, France, the British Isles, Cyprus, Crete, Sicily.
5.   Color in red the area of the Ottoman Empire *ca.* 1500.
6.   Color in yellow the area of the Papal States.
7.   Show in green the area of the Holy Roman Empire.
8.   Locate with a black dot and label Istanbul (Constantinople), Naples, Rome, Venice, Florence, Genoa, Milan, Pisa, Bologna.
9.   Show in blue the area of the Venetian Republic.
     (Duplicate the blank map to complete 8 and 9.)

II.   **READING THE MAP**

1.   What is the approximate distance in miles from Istanbul to Venice?
2.   Florence is located in the _____ of Italy on the _____ River.
3.   Genoa developed as a major port city in _____ Italy.
4.   The city of Venice is located at the _____ of the _____ Sea.
5.   Milan in the _____ of Italy was largely a _____-based power focused on _____.
6.   The position of the Italian Peninsula was a major factor in the commerce between Europe and the _____.

III.   **UNDERSTANDING THE MAP**

1.   Who were the main competitors for the Venetians in the eastern Mediterranean?
2.   The prosperity of Renaissance Italy involved wartime commerce with what regions?
3.   What was the major region to the north which provided economic opportunity for Italy during the Renaissance era?
4.   In general what was the fate of Italy in the fifteenth and sixteenth centuries?
5.   How would you describe the political character of the Papal States?
6.   Compare the general demographic character of Renaissance Italy with Central and Western Europe.

Exercise 27: Renaissance Italy: 1400-1600

400 Miles

400 Kilometers

0°

10°E

20°E

30°E

40°N

50°N

60°N

XXVIII. DISCOVERY AND EXPLORATION I: AFRICA

In the late fourteenth century and throughout the fifteenth century, the Portuguese took the lead in exploration and commercial enterprise outside Europe. Their Atlantic orientation and maritime and navigational technology allowed them to open new opportunities in Africa, Asia, and the New World. Initially, one of the major goals of African exploration was to find alternative routes to the East and bypass the Arab Islamic presence in North Africa and the Sahara regions. The Portuguese sought to exploit the supplies of pepper, gold, ivory, and, eventually, the slaves to be found in these areas. After establishing bases in northwest Africa, they ranged down the west coast around the Cape of Good Hope. From here they moved up the east coast of the continent and across the Arabian Sea and Indian Ocean to India and Southeast Asia. Eventually, they set up relations in China at Macao and in Japan at Nagasaki. Arabs, Persians, and even the Chinese had penetrated the east coast of Africa long before Arab traders and Islam, in particular, had been a force in this region.

The Atlantic coast, however, was virtually unknown to Europeans. The efforts to bypass the trans-Saharan trade and to tap Africa's markets and spread Christianity were promoted by the Portuguese monarchy. The Portuguese moved around Cape Bojador, acquired the Canaries and Madeira Islands and moved into the Guinea Coast area of Africa. In the Gulf, Sao Thomé, Princepe, and then El Mina came to be important bases for their operations. The Portuguese pattern was to deal with the indigenous population by trade or by force rather than to settle in large numbers or move very far inland. In some areas (i.e., Oyo and Benin) a complex regional trade system developed. European products such as cloth and tools were exchanged for slaves and gold. Slaves might be transported to Europe or used locally for the mines or sugar plantations.

The Portuguese impact on East Africa was dramatic and disruptive. They sought royal monopolies with force. They introduced new methods and new goals into a centuries-old commercial process. Their seizure of Sofala and Kilwa allowed them to dominate the gold trade center of Zimbabwe. Ginger, cinnamon, pepper, and silk were other products they controlled directly or through tolls from other carriers. Their fortress at Mozambique was a valuable post on the way to the Arabian Sea in their competition with the Moslems. Hormuz, at the entrance to the Persian Gulf, was a major fortress to secure that area. These advances would be matched by Diu and Goa in India.

Portuguese interest in the New World had an important African connection as well. Brazil lay due east of the Tordesillas line and, thus, came into the Portuguese orbit. After the mid sixteenth century Brazil became a focus for settlement and exploitation. It soon became the major area of sugar production, eclipsing the Spanish and earlier Portuguese enterprises off the African coast. Cheap slaves from the Congo and Angola were used in a well-organized plantation economy. The harsh methods of slave labor and control created a continuous demand for more. The slave trade had a serious impact on the source nations in various ways. Slaves were a source of income and also a labor supply for local enterprises. Slaves were used on plantations in Africa, and in the administrative bureaucracy and the military in Congo, ruled from Sao Salvador. The desire for still more slaves and silver from the interior led the Portuguese to conquer Angola. Angola was administered from the coastal city of Luanda.

EXERCISE 28
DISCOVERY AND EXPLORATION I: AFRICA

I.   MAKING THE MAP

1.   Locate and label the Mediterranean Sea, the Atlantic Ocean, the Red Sea, the Gulf of Guinea, the Nile River, the Senegal River, the Niger River, the Congo River, the Zambezi River, Lake Chad, Lake Victoria, Lake Tanganyika.

2.   Locate and label the Azores Islands, the Canary Islands, Kilwa, Zanzibar, Lao Tome, Madagascar, Principe, Cape of Good Hope, the Sahara Desert, Arabia, Guinea, Mali, Angola, Sudan, Ghana, Songhay, Ivory Coast, Slave Coast, Gold Coast, Changamire, Maravi.

3.   Locate with a black dot and label Sijilmasa, Timbuktu, Elmina, Sao Salvador, Luanda, Sofala, Tete, Mozambique, Mombasa, Aden.

4.   Show in blue the area of Oyo, in red the area of Benin, in yellow the area of Congo, in orange the area of the Mwenemutapa, and the line of the Equator.

II.   READING THE MAP

1.   What is the approximate distance in miles from Sijilmasa to Timbuktu?

2.   European explorers had to navigate around and beyond what promontory in West Africa to reach areas to the south?

3.   Name the groups of islands off the west coast of Africa discovered and controlled by Europeans in the fifteenth century.

4.   An important base for Portuguese economic exploitation of the Gold Coast was _____.

5.   Two islands vital to Portuguese activity in Equatorial Africa were _____ and _____, located in the Gulf of _____.

6.   The Canary Islands and Madeira were developed by the Portuguese for what purposes?

7.   Portuguese success in East Africa and the Indian Ocean was secured through control of the port of _____, the city of _____, and the fortress on _____ Island.

8.   Moslem rivals to Portuguese maritime activity in the Indian Ocean operated from the port city of _____ in _____ Arabia.

III.   UNDERSTANDING THE MAP

1.   At the beginning of the fifteenth century, what region in Africa was free of outside penetration?

2.   What was the major initial motivation behind Portuguese efforts to circumnavigate Africa?

3. What commodities were the Portuguese seeking in West Africa and who were their competitors in that region?

4. Name some of the technological innovations crucial to European maritime exploration and commercial development.

5. What commodity from West Africa came to be vital to the economic development of areas outside Africa?

6. What was the line of demarcation of the Treaty of Tordesillas and how did it affect Portuguese possessions?

7. In what areas of East Asia did the Portuguese establish trading posts?

8. In what region of the New World did the Portuguese have territorial possessions and how was it significantly different from its other colonies?

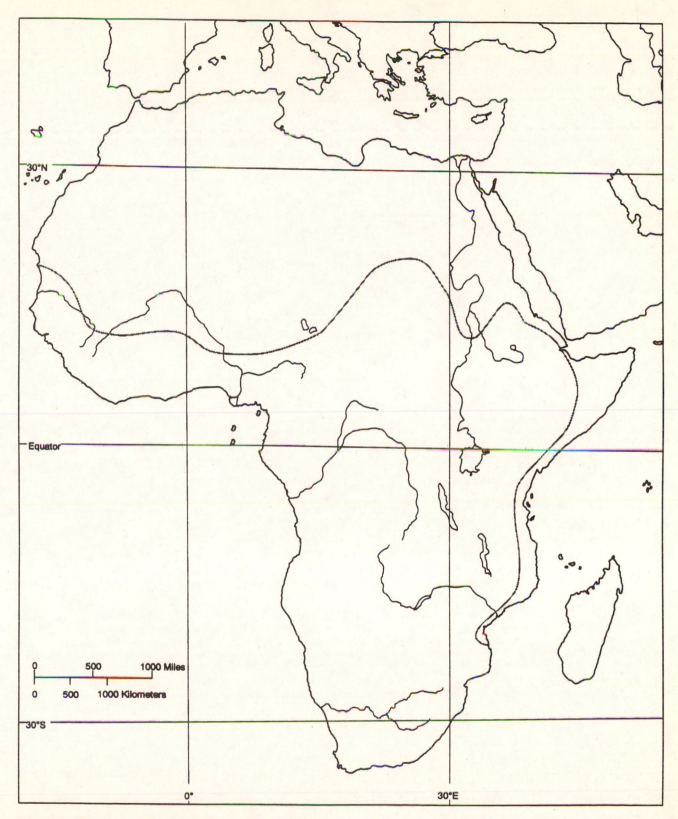

Exercise 28: Discovery and Exploration I: Africa

XXIX. DISCOVERY AND EXPLORATION II: "THE NEW WORLD"

In their search for alternative routes to the East, the Spanish chose to sail west around the globe. Their miscalculations on the distance involved resulted in some major surprises and discoveries. Even after reaching land which they named Hispaniola, they continued in the belief that China lay just beyond. They crossed not only the great expanse of the Atlantic Ocean, but eventually discovered a second even larger ocean, the Pacific. The Pacific lay beyond the previously unknown great land masses of North and South America. In addition, of course, there was the revelation that these vast regions were populated by a variety of indigenous peoples some of whom were organized into powerful centralized states.

This "New World" would quickly become the object of exploitation, settlement, and a major area of international competition involving the Spanish, Portuguese, English, Dutch, and French. The sea lanes to and from these areas, the coastal passages, and the interior, were completely transformed over the sixteenth and seventeenth centuries. The Spanish were the leaders in Middle and South America. The Portuguese opened Brazil after the Tordesillas Treaty of 1494. Initially, they competed with French interests, there, but went on to create the Western world's largest sugar-producing operation. They drew directly on their colony in Angola for slave labor. Subsequently, the English and Dutch would focus on the north in a futile search for still another route to the East.

Initially, the main focus of the Spanish was in the Isthmus, Mexico, and Peru. These expeditions effectively overcame the organized opposition of American-Indian regimes such as the Incas and Aztecs, and instituted governments in the name of the Spanish kings. In most instances, the Indian population was virtually enslaved or reduced to serfdom. Acapulco on the west coast of Mexico was developed as a port for shipping on to Manila and Luzon in the Philippines. Silk was brought from the Far East in exchange for New World silver. A chain of fortified harbors was established for shipment of gold and silver back to Spain. Armed convoys put out from Cartagena on the Gulf of Uraba, Veracruz in Mexico, and San Juan in Puerto Rico.

Wars, slavery, and especially disease destroyed much of the native population. European settlers and slaves from Africa added new elements to the linguistic and cultural mix which emerged in successive generations. The surviving indigenous population persisted and inter-married with Europeans and Africans. Cuba, Brazil, and Haiti were among the regions where larger numbers of African were settled as slaves.

Silver, gold, jewels, cattle, and sugar-cane came to be the main products extracted from the New World. Cities such as Potosi in the Andes prospered in the areas where there was mining of precious gems, gold, and silver. Large agricultural estates produced cattle, sugar cane, and tobacco. The plantation type of economy not only increased production but opened the market for the African slave trade. The Spanish Crown controlled the exploitation of its new territories so as to bring in the greatest possible benefit. Shipping was strictly regulated and restricted to Seville in Spain, and Veracruz and Panama in the New World. The system proved cumbersome, inefficient and, in the end, had an inflationary effect at home and abroad. Spain continued to rely on the English and Dutch markets for manufacture and never developed a solid urban middle class or commercial community. Piracy, privateering, and smuggling took a considerable toll on the bullion shipments. In addition, the Anglo-Spanish conflict of the late sixteenth century seriously diminished Spanish naval power. However, at the same time the Crowns of Spain and Portugal were joined. This linked the Spanish American and Indian Ocean interests, as well as the Afro-Brazilian sugar enterprise.

Overall the effect on the indigenous populations of Africa, North, Middle, and South America was, of course, devastating. The blessings of discovery came at a high price. And even the benefits extracted by the imperial powers brought little to their own people at large and the capital was eventually squandered and exhausted.

EXERCISE 29
DISCOVERY AND EXPLORATION II: "THE NEW WORLD"

I. **MAKING THE MAP**

   1.   Locate and label the Pacific Ocean, Atlantic Ocean, Gulf of Mexico, Caribbean Sea, Cape Horn, Strait of Magellan.
   2.   Locate and label the Andes Mountains, Amazon River, Orinoco River, the Equator, the Tropic of Capricorn.
   3.   Locate and label Cuba, Haiti, the Dominican Republic, Yucatan Peninsula, Puerto Rico, the Sierra Madre Mountains.
   4.   Locate with a black dot and label Buenos Aires, Cuzco, Machu Picchu, Quito, Chichén Itzá, Tikal, Chiapas, Tenochitlan.
   5.   Color in red the area of Brazil.
   6.   Color in yellow the area of the Aztec Empire.
   7.   Color in blue the area of the Inca Empire.
   8.   Show the line of the Tordesillas Treaty demarcation line.
        (Duplicate the blank map to complete 5-8.)

II. **READING THE MAP**

   1.   The approximate distance in miles from Lisbon to Rio de Janeiro is _____.
   2.   What is the distance in miles from Seville to Vera Cruz?
   3.   The Amazon River, located in _____, runs generally from _____ to _____ and empties into the _____ Ocean.
   4.   The predominant natural feature of the interior of Brazil is _____.
   5.   The most prominent geological feature of the west coast region of South America is _____.
   6.   Through what modern South American nation does the line of the Equator run?

III. **UNDERSTANDING THE MAP**

   1.   Describe the general features of the demographic changes in Middle and South America that resulted from European penetration of these regions.
   2.   What organized states confronted the Spanish conquistadors in Middle and South America?
   3.   What natural barrier limited Incan expansion to the east of Quito and Cuzco?
   4.   Describe the importance of the city of Tenochtitlan to the Aztec Empire.
   5.   Discuss the natural features of Brazil that made it difficult to administer for the Portuguese authorities.
   6.   List the major products that the Spanish and Portuguese sought in their new world territories.

7. What was the crucial element that connected Portuguese exploitation of Brazil with her territories in Africa?
8. What were the three cities through which all Spanish-New World trade was required to pass?
9. Name the nations that came to rival Portuguese and Spanish interests in the New World.

Exercise 29: Discovery and Exploration II: "The New World"

XXX. THE ISLAMIC WORLD: THE OTTOMAN EMPIRE

The Ottoman Turks, who established their empire in the fourteenth and fifteenth centuries, were heirs to a great warrior tradition. Osman I (d. 1326) was the leader of a warrior group originally allied to the Seljuk Turks. Osman founded a movement which reinvigorated Islam and set out to build a universal empire. He renewed the Seljuk war on the Byzantine Empire which dated to the eleventh century. The Seljuk Turks or Rum Seljuks were the western-most branch of Central Asian nomadic warriors such as the Great Seljuks in western Persia and the Ghaznevids in Afghanistan and northwest India. Virtually all of Asia Minor came under the control of these militant nomads. Initially, they ruled from Bursa near the Sea of Marmara. They were set in motion in part by the Mongols' westward movement in the thirteenth century. Their warrior ideals were reinforced with religious enthusiasm and the drive for conquest and loot. Their military effectiveness was also enhanced by the use of firearms. From Asia Minor they moved into the troubled Byzantine Empire's European provinces to position their assault on Constantinople. From Adrianople (Edirne) they moved into the Balkan states of Bulgaria, Macedonia, Bosnia, and Serbia.

The Ottoman defeat of the Serbs at Kosovo in 1389 allowed them to advance to the Danube where they threatened Wallachia. In 1396 a Western rescue force was defeated at Nicopolis. However, a second Mongol advance led by Timur the Lame (Tammerlane) dealt the Turks a serious blow at Ankara, delaying the assault on Constantinople. Timur had in mind a second Mongol Empire but that scheme ended with his death in 1405.

Mehmet II (d. 1481) completed the conquest of the Byzantine Empire in 1453 with the capture of Constantinople. Only Trebizond on the south shore of the Black Sea held out until 1461. Elsewhere, in Syria, Egypt and the Levant the Turks were victorious. Kurdistan, in northern Mesopotamia, rounded out its territories in that region. The Crimea marked the limit of its power beyond the northern shores of the Black Sea. To the west, the Turks nearly reached the Strait of Gibraltar along the shores of North Africa. In 1480 they destroyed the city of Otranto in southern Italy.

Under Selim (d. 1520) and Suleiman the Magnificent (d. 1566) further gains were made as Albania, Serbia, and Bosnia became provinces. Beyond the Danube, Wallachia and Moldavia were forced to pay tribute. Transylvania and Hungary fell after the battle of Mohacs in 1526. The fall of Belgrade in 1521 opened the way to further westward conquest. Vienna itself was beseiged in 1529. The attack on Vienna and the destruction of Otranto probably are high-water marks or even overextensions of Turkish expansion. But in the eastern Mediterranean the Venetians and Genoese had to make concessions, especially after the fall of Rhodes and then Cyprus. The Holy League, composed of the papacy, Spain, and Venice, resisted the Turks and their European ally, France. At Lepanto in 1571 the Turks were dealt a serious setback.

To the east, Suleiman consolidated his successes with the capture of Baghdad and the control of western Persia. At its peak in the mid-sixteenth century there was no larger empire in the world. Suleiman ruled from Constantinople, which had been renamed Istanbul. This great city, now rebuilt and embellished, was greater in size and splendor than Rome, Florence, Paris, or Baghdad. It was the center of a largely self-sufficient empire which drew on its province tributaries and vassals for food-stuffs, luxuries, slaves, and recruits for the army. The Turkish Empire effectively blocked and controlled the traditional east-west overland and Mediterranean trade routes. But there was extensive, indirect international trade. Paris, London, Florence, Cairo, Salonica, and Baghdad were all a part of this complicated network. Eventually, of course, Europeans sought alternative routes and markets.

Ottoman sultans ruled with a strong hand, with their standing army and elite Janissaries as their primary force. They drew heavily on Greek and Slavic elements in an administrative system which parcelled out authority for military and fiscal tasks. Much of the governmental apparatus was carried over from Byzantine or Persian patterns. A measure of tolerance and freedom from forced conversion to Islam were traded for obedience and tribute payment, after the worst excesses during the period of conquest in the fourteenth century.

EXERCISE 30
THE ISLAMIC WORLD: THE OTTOMAN EMPIRE

I.   **MAKING THE MAP**

1. Locate and label the Mediterranean Sea, the Red Sea, the Persian Gulf, the Black Sea, the Caspian Sea.
2. Locate and label the Tigris River, the Euphrates River, the Nile River, the Danube River.
3. Locate and label the Safavid Empire, Arabia, Egypt, Anatolia, Italy, the Sharifian Empire.
4. Locate and label Syria, Maghreb, Bosnia, Serbia, Andalus, Hungary, Wallachia.
5. Locate with a black dot and label Baghdad, Ankara, Cairo, Tripoli, Algiers, Rome, Venice, Vienna, Buda, Istanbul, Mecca, Manzikert, Bari.
6. Show in green the European territory of the Ottoman Empire *ca.* 1500.
7. Show in red the Ottoman territory in North Africa excluding the vassal states.
8. Show in red the territory of the Ottoman Empire from Anatolia to the east and south.
   (Duplicate the blank map to complete 6-8.)

II.   **READING THE MAP**

1. What is the approximate distance in miles from Baghdad to Istanbul?
2. What is the approximate distance in miles from Istanbul to Vienna?
3. What river formed, in part, the border between Ottoman Europe and the empire's tributary states there?
4. In what regions in the north of the Black Sea did the Ottoman Turks establish their power?
5. Name the three large islands in the eastern Mediterranean Sea which fell to Ottoman control?

III.   **UNDERSTANDING THE MAP**

1. What empire collapsed as a result of Ottoman expansion in Anatolia and southeastern Europe?
2. What were the tributary territories of the Ottoman Empire in Eastern Europe?
3. What kingdoms fell under Ottoman rule in southeastern Europe?
4. Name the major threat on the eastern border of the Ottoman Empire which was a concern as the Ottoman Turks pushed into Europe.
5. Islamic expansion in Eastern Europe was counterbalanced by the major loss of what other area in Europe by 1500?
6. What elements limited Turkish expansion in Europe?

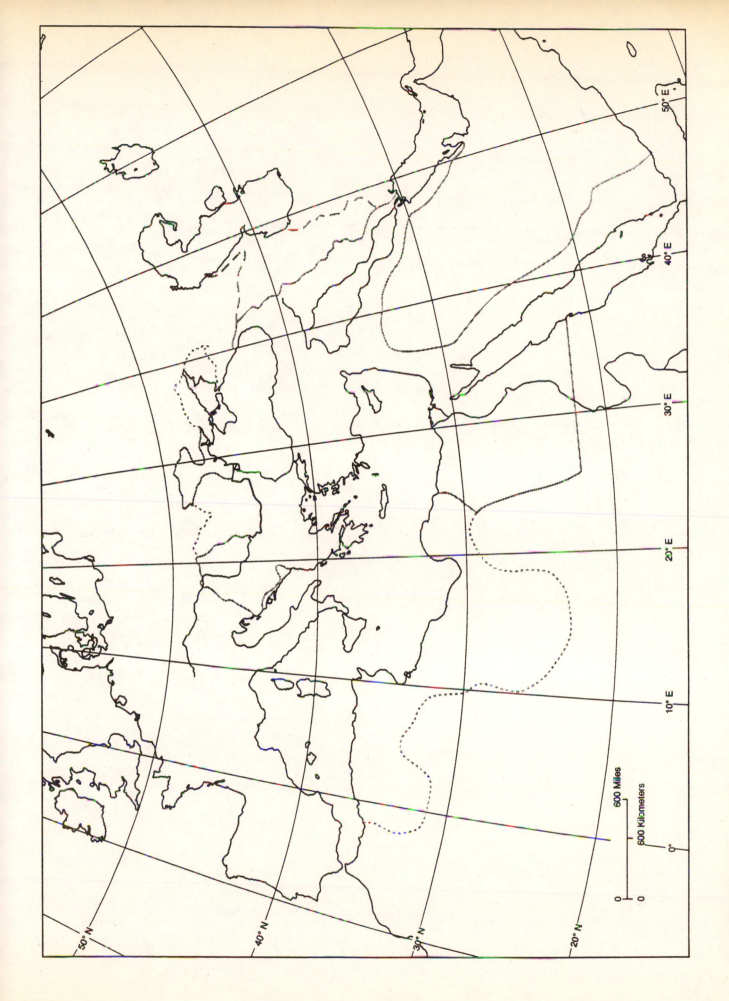

Exercise 30: The Islamic World: The Ottoman Empire

50° E

40° E

30° E

20° E

10° E

0°

50° N

40° N

30° N

20° N

600 Miles

600 Kilometers

0

0

XXXI. THE WORLD OF ISLAM: IRAN, INDIA, AND NORTH AFRICA

Safavid Persia (Iran) was one of the three powerful Turk-based Islamic empires of the fourteenth, fifteenth, and sixteenth centuries. It was, in fact, located between the other two: the Ottoman Turks centered in Istanbul, and Mughal India, administered from Delhi and Agra. Seljuk Turks had appeared in Persia in the eleventh century. Two Mongol assaults devastated the region in the thirteenth and fourteenth centuries. The Safavids, also from central Asia, became the political power in Persia under Ismail (d. 1524). His range included Armenia, Azerbaijan, and Iraq. This Empire extended from the Oxus River south to the Arabian Sea. The capital was at Isfahan. With a population of about sixty thousand, it became a great cultural and economic center. During Ismail's son's long reign, the territory was successfully defended against Ottoman Turks, the major threat from the west.

The empire reached its peak under Shah Abbas the Great (d. 1629). It was well administered, prosperous, and proved to be one of the greatest eras of Persian culture. An efficient network of roads connected the cities and facilitated commerce and administrative efficiency. Overland trade connected the Caspian Sea and the Persian Gulf where the Safavids were a major presence. The Persian gulf ports allowed them, as well as Europeans, to bypass the Ottoman Empire. India was subject to Islamic elements through Arab contacts in the eighth century. Central Asian Turks brought the next wave of invaders, in the eleventh century, from the area of northwest India.

Up through the fifteenth century one Turkic or Turkic-Afghan group after another established itself in India. The invasion of Timur (Tamerlane, d. 1405) was one of the most destructive and ruthless. It effectively put an end to the Delhi Sultanate which was founded in the early thirteenth century. Chaotic political and economic conditions brought Babur (d. 1530) into India from his base in Afghanistan. This victory at Panipat in the Punjab, near Delhi, opened the way to the founding of the Mughal or Mogul Empire.

Under Babur and Akban (d. 1605) disunity was overcome to create a large, powerful, and efficient empire. Agricultural and commercial enterprises provided staples and revenues for a population of one hundred million. Delhi and Agra served as twin capitals. Under Akbar, Rajput, Gugerat, Bengal, and Afghanistan were incorporated into the empire. The territory stretched from the Himalaya Range in the north to the Godavari River in the south. The Brahmaputra River was the borderline to the east. Along the shores of the Indian Ocean important contacts were made in the west of Diu in the Gugerat, Daman, Goa, and south to Calicut. Colombo in Ceylon was another important port. The Portuguese, Dutch, English, French, and Danes, seeking textiles, sugar, and indigo, maintained trading posts in these locations. The Mughal sultans ruled their lands as tribute states, provinces, or allies with an efficient bureaucratic administration.

The Sharafian Islamic State evolved from a long struggle in Northwest Africa. Here a Sharafian dynasty, which traced itself to Mohammed, put together a powerful force combining strong leadership, religious zeal, and military skills. In their period of greatest strength, the powerful leaders drew on the support of Sufism which had deep roots in the Moroccan population. This was the only region in North Africa free from Ottoman control which included most of the rest of the Maghreb—Algeria, Tunisia, and Libya.

The Spanish and Portuguese had designs on the region as well, following the Reconquista which drove Islam from the Iberian Peninsula at the end of the fifteenth century. The Portuguese were active along the Atlantic shores of western North Africa, with a focus on Tangier, but were driven out of Morocco. Europeans were particularly interested in the gold and slave supplies from West Africa. The Sharafians were able to control much of that trade from Fez and Timbuktu, deeper into the hinterland. Their centralized government was based on the Ottoman administrative mode and was quite effective. Here, as with the Ottoman Turks, the Safavids and Mughals were able to draw on the West's economic resurgence. The increased population and available capital made for tremendous markets.

EXERCISE 31
THE WORLD OF ISLAM: IRAN, INDIA, AND NORTH AFRICA

I. **MAKING THE MAP**

1. Locate and label the Pacific Ocean, the Indian Ocean, the Bay of Bengal, the Arabian Sea, the Atlantic Ocean, the Mediterranean Sea, the Red Sea, the Black Sea, the Caspian Sea.
2. Locate and label the Ganges River, the Indus River, the Tigris River, the Euphrates River, the Nile River, the Danube River.
3. Locate and label the Sahara Desert, Africa, Spain, Italy, Anatolia, Arabia, Iraq, Iran, India.
4. Color in green the area of the Ottoman Empire *ca.* 1500.
5. Show in red the area of the Safavid Empire.
6. Show in blue the area of the Sharafian Empire.
7. Show in orange the area of the Mughal Empire.
8. Locate with a black dot and label Samarkand, Delhi, Lahore, Kabul, Calicut, Isfahan, Timbuktu, Sijilmasa, Tangier, Istanbul, Baghdad, Cairo, Damascus. (Duplicate the blank map to complete 4-7.)

II. **READING THE MAP**

1. What was the name of the territories that made up the Empire of the Safavids?
2. What power blocked Safavid expansion to the west?
3. What was the capital of the Safavid Empire?
4. At its peak, the Mughal Empire which extended from the _____ mountains in the north into central India, was an area known as the _____.
5. The Sharifian Empire, located in _____ Africa, extended from the city of _____ south to _____.
6. In addition to North Africa, the other important area of Islamic influence on that continent was the _____ coast on the shores of the _____.

III. **UNDERSTANDING THE MAP**

1. In what region did the Safavid power originate?
2. What power was the major rival to Safavids in the region to the west?
3. What city served as the early base of power for the founders of the Mughal dynasty?
4. What was the political situation in India when the Mughal forces appeared under Babur?
5. Who were the major European rivals to the Sharifians in northwest Africa in the fifteenth and sixteenth centuries?
6. Outside of Algiers, what were the cities key to Sharifian political and economic power?

153

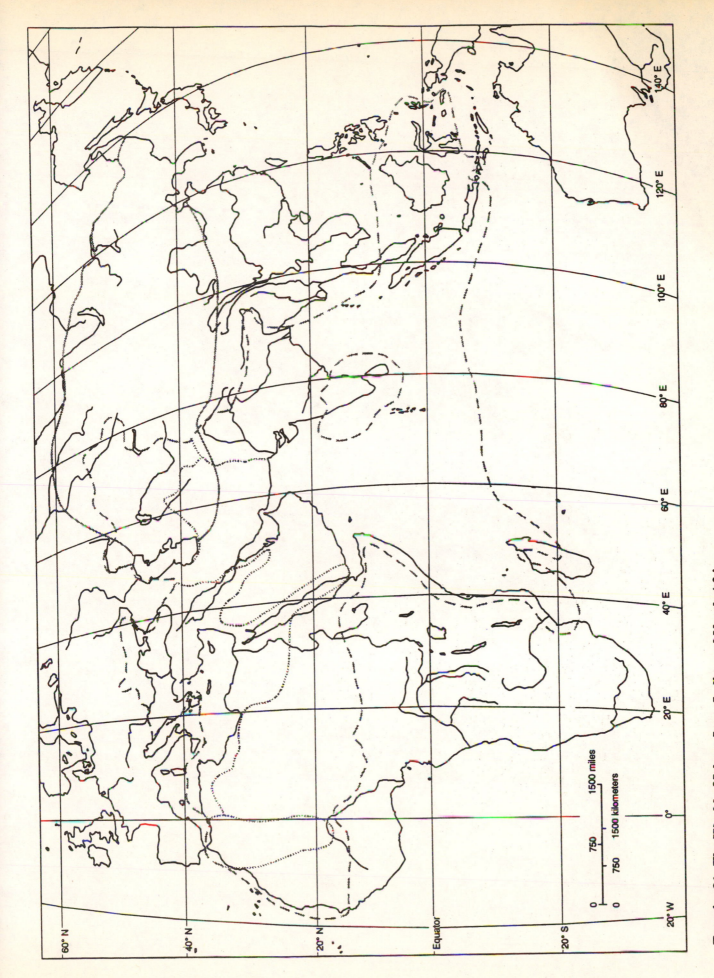

Exercise 31: The World of Islam: Iran, India, and North Africa

155

XXXII. THE WORLD OF ISLAM: INDIA AND SOUTHEAST ASIA

Quite different patterns emerged in northern and southern India between the eleventh and sixteenth centuries. Northern India fell prey to the aggressive Turco-Afghans such as Mahmud of Ghazni (d. 1030). An empire that included Punjab, Hindustan, and Bengal, was ruled from the capital at Delhi. It was established in the early thirteenth century as the Delhi Sultanate. Continued factionalism among the various peoples of India prevented any effective resistance to a series of sultanates down to 1526. The Deccan Plateau remained beyond their reach except for raiding parties. The Delhi sultans were strong enough to resist the Mongol invasion of the fourteenth century under Al-ud-din-Khalji (d. 1316). The Tughluqs continued the process of spreading Islam in India and renewed expeditions into the Deccan. They met their match with Tamerlane (Timur) the Mongol. He captured Delhi and left the Punjab in ruins. In the aftermath of the Mongol assault, the Lodi Afghan clan controlled Delhi until challenged in the territories of the sultanate. It was the dissension in the empire that brought Babur, a new conqueror, into India.

South India was dominated by Pandya on the southern tip of India. It was administered from Madurai. Just to the north of Pandya was Chola which came to be an important maritime power with strong contacts in Southeast Asia. The Chola fleet also had a considerable role in the island of Ceylon. The Cholas were challenged by both the Pandyans and the Sinhalese in Ceylon in the late thirteenth century. Beyond Chola territory, the Pallavan dynasty was another example of an independent indigenous state. It was the Vijayanagar Empire that emerged in a response to Delhi Sultanate raids into the region. In the fourteenth century they went on to organize much of the area of the south. The capital, also called Vijayanagar, was a large impressive city in the fifteenth and sixteenth centuries until its capture and destruction by the Mughals from northern India.

In addition to the mainland states of Burma (Myanmar), Cambodia, Laos, Siam (Thailand) and Vietnam, Southeast Asia includes a number of island nations located between the Asian mainland and Australia to the south. These islands are spread over thousands of miles, from the Indian Ocean to the Coral Sea, to the east, and from the Philippine Sea, south, near the shores of Australia. The South China Sea separates them from the Asian mainland. The Philippines, to the north, are made up of some 7,100 islands. Java, Sumatra, and Borneo are among the larger islands of the group known as Indonesia. Altogether Indonesia includes 13,667 islands.

The long narrow Malay Peninsula is politically and culturally connected to the islands more than to the mainland. The region more or less straddles the Equator so that the climate is hot and humid. Much of the land is mountainous, heavily forested, or swampy. The economy can vary from simple hunting-gathering in the mountain regions to maritime commerce, very important in a region that is one of the world's major crossroads.

The Malaccan Strait between the Malay Peninsula and Sumatra was a major passageway but it was rivaled by the Sunda Strait between Java and Sumatra. The region, as a whole, lacks political and cultural cohesion and was often subject to influences and domination or exploitation from more powerful states. A great variety of indigenous cultures, languages, and patterns did persist, however. The New Guinea group of over six hundred islands, comparable to the state of California in land area, for instance, has over seven hundred different linguistic groups.

Pre-Islamic Arab traders were active in this region very early. There were strong ties between East Asia and the Indian Ocean as well. One early state was that of Sri Vijaya. Another was Sailendra.

At this time in the eighth century there were strong influences from India. In the eleventh century Chola in south India was a major competitor in the area. Much of the Indonesian region was incorporated into the kingdom of Majapahit in the mid-fourteenth century.

By 1400, the new state of Malacca emerged with a strong Moslem element from North India. Islam, along with Hinduism and Buddhism, brought by missionaries and traders, had a strong influence in the area. Malacca on the Malay Peninsula and the Islamic areas of northern Sumatra and Java became rich and powerful in the agriculture and maritime commerce of the region. Rice, spices, timber, and textiles were some of the sought-after products. They extended their operations north and east to Mindanao in the Philippines. There they would eventually face stiff competition from Europeans.

EXERCISE 32
THE WORLD OF ISLAM: INDIA AND SOUTHEAST ASIA

I. MAKING THE MAP

1. Locate and label the Arabian Sea, the Indian Ocean, the Bay of Bengal, the South China Sea, the Pacific Ocean, the Gulf of Siam, the Sulu Sea, the Celebes Sea, the Malacca Straits.
2. Locate and label the Indus River, the Ganges River, the Brahmaputra River, the Irrawaddy River, the Mekong River.
3. Locate and label the Hindu Kush, the Tibetan Plateau, the Great Indian Desert, the Himalaya Mountains, the Deccan Plateau, Ceylon, the Philippine Islands.
4. Locate with a black dot and label Delhi, Benares, Calicut, Kandy, Mandalay, Rangoon, Bangkok, Angkor, Jogjakata (Jakarta).
5, Locate and label Bali, Timor, Borneo, Tibet.
6. Show in blue the area of the Delhi Sultanate *ca.* 1236.
7. Locate and label the Sind, Punjab, Bengal, Vijayanagar, Chola.
8. Show in yellow the area of the Empire of the Tughluqs in the fourteenth century.
9. Locate and label the area of Burma, Siam, Cambodia, Vietnam, Malaya, Sumatra, Java, Mindanao, Laos.
   (Duplicate the blank map to complete 6-9.)

II. READING THE MAP

1. The Indian subcontinent was invaded by Islamic elements in the eleventh century from the area of _____.
2. The Turco-Afghan empire in India had its capital at _____ and stretched from the _____ River in the west to the _____ in the east.
3. The two threats to the Delhi Sultanate from outside India in the fourteenth century came from the _____ and _____.
4. What natural barrier limited Delhi's control of south India?
5. What is the name of the large island southeast of India across the Indian Ocean?
6. What is the approximate distance in miles from India to Mindanao?

III. UNDERSTANDING THE MAP

1. What conditions existed in post-Gupta-Harsha India which facilitated invasion and conquest?
2. By what means was Islamic religion and culture spread to Southeast Asia in the fifteenth and sixteenth centuries?
3. What western powers would challenge Islamic expansion in Southeast Asia in the fifteenth and sixteenth centuries?
4. In what two modern nations of the Indian subcontinent are the greatest concentrations of Moslems to be found today?
5. In what regions of Southeast Asia did Islam make a permanent impact?

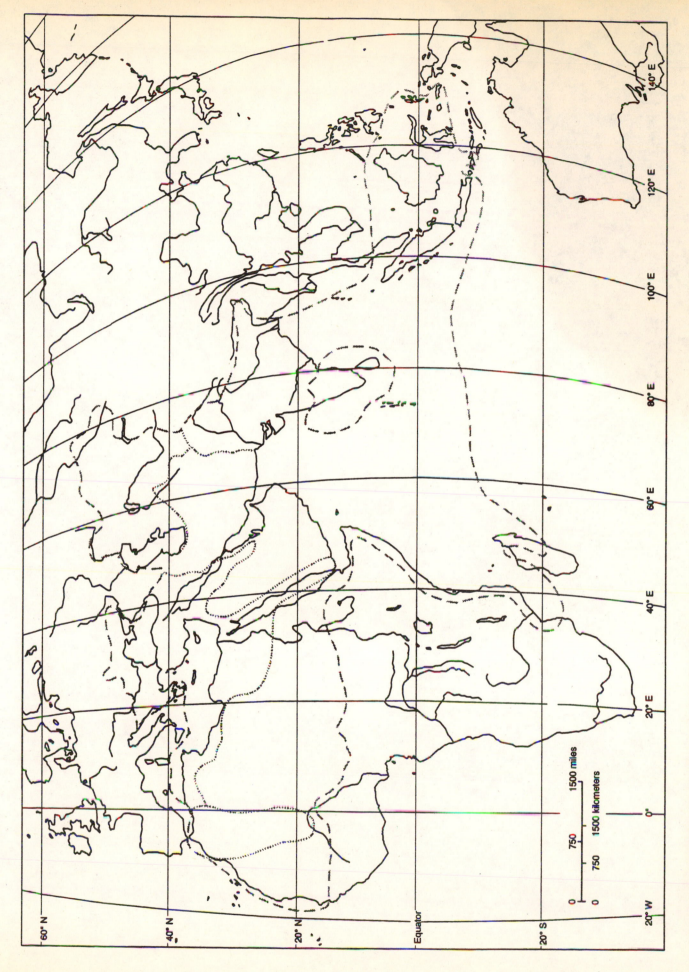

60° N

40° N

20° N

Equator

20° S

20° W

0°

20° E

40° E

60° E

80° E

100° E

120° E

140° E

0 750 1500 miles

0 750 1500 kilometers

Exercise 32: The World of Islam: India and Southeast Asia

161

Over the course of the last half of the sixteenth century, Europe was caught up in a series of struggles by absolutist monarchs. Spain, in particular, felt obliged to assert itself against the English and French. The Netherlands and Italy became battlegrounds in dynastic and religious issues. Dynastic interests and religious enthusiasm were behind a great deal of Spain's actions under Charles V and Philip II. Charles V, as King of Spain and Holy Roman Emperor, saw himself at the head of a Universal Christian Empire. In the East, his main enemy was another empire: that of the Islamic Ottoman Turks. The Ottoman Empire had overrun much of Eastern Europe and even besieged Vienna (1529). In the West as well, Spain had to contend with the Turks and their sometime ally the French. In the 1520s Italy was ravaged by this struggle which often saw the papacy opposing the emperor. The issues were further muddled by the religious issues raised by Protestants in Europe, and the Church of England. Charles's other concern was the power of the princes in Germany. Here the insistence upon traditional political liberties and religious issues often combined to oppose his authority. Philip II took up the cause of Universal Empire (1556–1598) and faced a variety of problems. The French and the English opposed him in Europe and in the New World. The Holy League did limit Turkish expansion in the Mediterranean with the defeat of the Ottoman fleet at Lepanto off the west coast of Greece in 1571. Another success under Philip was the union with Portugal in 1580, but the defeat of the Great Armada in 1588 by the English was a major setback in Spanish power and prestige. Political rivalry, religious zeal, and English support of the Dutch were major factors in the Spanish-English conflict. The long and costly struggle to control The Netherlands took its toll on Spain. First the northern sections broke away and eventually all the seventeen provinces freed themselves (1648) to form a republic. This region with over two hundred prosperous cities had been a major source of income to the Spanish Crown. Rotterdam and Antwerp controlled close to fifty percent of the world's trade. Within a century Spain, which once had the most extensive territories, the greatest income, and Europe's best army and navy, was on the path to decline.

The French succeeded in creating a strong centralized absolutist monarchy. French monarchs survived internal challenges from the nobility, the threats from Spain, and the Huguenot Protestants. With the beginning of challenges to Spanish power at the end of the sixteenth century, France was poised to become a major power on the continent under Louis XIV. The English under the Tudors were largely successful in bringing territorial integrity to their island kingdom by the reign of Elizabeth (d. 1603). Scotland was the exception to that general picture. England successfully challenged Spain and went on to develop her own overseas interests in the East and the New World.

Russia, under Ivan IV (d. 1584), saw the attempt to centralize administrative power and expand territorially. Ivan ruthlessly suppressed any opposition from the nobles. He expanded to the south against the khanates of Kajan and Astrakhan, as far as the region of the Caspian, and the territory of the Ottoman Turks in the Black Sea-Crimean area. He opened the conquest of Siberia, to the east, and established a seaport at Archangel on the White Sea. His extended efforts in the west, in Livonia, ended in failure. Here Russia, Poland, and the Swedes competed in the vital region of the Baltic Sea. With the death of Ivan IV, his schemes for an Orthodox Empire and Russian unity collapsed in an internal power struggle. The Time of Troubles lasted until the foundation of the Romanov dynasty in 1613.

EXERCISE 33
EUROPE, *CA.* 1600

I.   MAKING THE MAP

1.   Locate and label the Atlantic Ocean, Mediterranean Sea, the Black Sea, the North Sea, the Baltic Sea, the English Channel.
2.   Locate and label the Rhine River, the Danube River, the Dnieper River, the Volga River.
3.   Locate and label the Papal States, Naples, the Ottoman Empire, France, Spain, England, Poland, Hungary, Lithuania, Muscovy, the Netherlands, Belgium.
4.   Locate and label Castile, Aragon, Burgundy, Navarre, Granada, Catalonia, Ireland, Scotland, Wales, Wallachia, Moldavia, Bohemia, the Crimean Khanate, Algiers, Tunis, the Mamluk Empire.
5.   Locate with a black dot and label Madrid, Lisbon, London, Rome, Istanbul, Venice, Vienna, Budapest, Milan, Paris, Moscow, Novgorod, Warsaw, Amsterdam, Antwerp, Utrecht.
6.   Show in red the area of the Holy Roman Empire *ca.* 1550.
7.   Show in blue the area of the Ottoman Empire *ca.* 1600.
8.   Show in orange the United Netherlands and Switzerland.
     (Dupicate the blank map to complete 5-8.)

II.   READING THE MAP

1.   In the fifteenth and sixteenth centuries Muscovy grew at the expense of the _____ Empire to the east and the _____ to the west.
2.   Poland benefitted from its port city of _____ on the _____ Sea.
3.   The main regions of the British Isles are _____, _____, _____, and _____.
4.   In the fifteenth and sixteenth centuries, the region of _____ was the major threat to unity and royal power in the British Isles.
5.   The marriage of Ferdinand and Isabella in Spain brought together the regions of _____ and _____.
6.   Two new political entities that emerged in the early seventeenth century which were a part of the Holy Roman Empire were _____ on the North Sea coast and _____ north of Italy.

III. UNDERSTANDING THE MAP

1.   What was the major preoccupation of the rulers of Muscovy/Russia in the areas to the west of their territory?
2.   What regions of the British Isles proved resistant to royal control in the fifteenth century?

3. Where was the major European battleground for English, French and Spanish rivalry in the sixteenth century?

4. In terms of territorial possessions, who were the most powerful monarchs of Europe in the late sixteenth and seventeenth centuries?

5. List some of the most important of those territories.

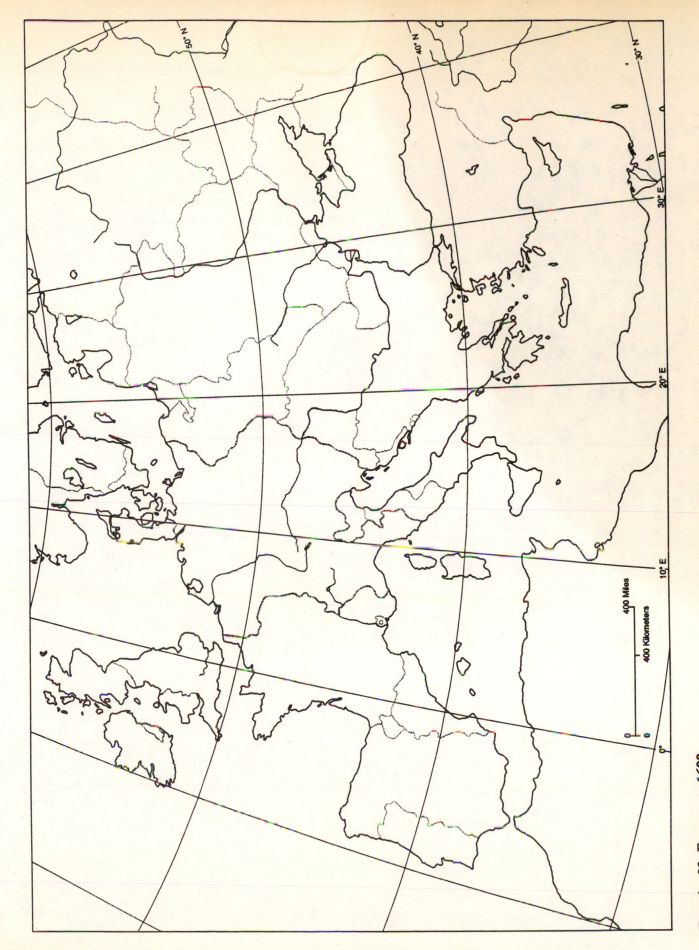

Exercise 33: Europe, ca 1600

400 Miles

400 Kilometers

50° N

40° N

30° N

30° E

20° E

10° E

0°